D0519125

PRACTICAL CHRISTIANITY TO-DAY
The Critic is Answered

The entire author's royalties from the sales of this book are being devoted to the Social Work of the West London Mission, Kingsway Hall, London, W.C.2.

PRACTICAL CHRISTIANITY TO-DAY

The Critic is Answered

by

THE REV. DR. DONALD O. SOPER

Twenty-five broadcast talks in the B.B.C. series
"Talking with You," and five People's Services,
printed with some alterations

With an Introduction by
The Rev. Kenneth Grayston
Acting Director of Religious Broadcasting, B.B.C.

KEN-PAX PUBLISHING CO LTD
KINGSWAY HALL
LONDON WC2

BOOK
PRODUCTION
WAR ECONOMY
STANDARD

THIS BOOK IS PRODUCED IN COMPLETE
CONFORMITY WITH THE AUTHORIZED
ECONOMY STANDARDS

Printed in Great Britain by Edgar G. Dunstan & Co.
Drayton House, Gordon Street, London, W.C.1

CONTENTS

CONTENTS

INTRODUCTION

RADIO'S job is communication. The most outstanding part (though not the whole) of communication is "getting something across". To do it effectively the broadcaster must be expert at his job, he must be sincere about what he is doing, and he must know his audience. That is true of every kind of broadcast, and of all the B.B.C.'s programmes. When the Light Programme came on the air in July 1945, the B.B.C. launched out on a policy of communication to a very wide audience. It was "designed to appeal not so much to a certain class of listener, but to all listeners when they are in certain moods". So, to a great extent, the attitudes, experiences, and needs of a great body of listeners dictated what should go into the programme. Yet at the same time Light Programme broadcasting had no intention of cutting itself off from the possibility of increasing the range of listeners' experiences. It set out to be entertaining and interesting in the widest possible sense.

The contribution of religious broadcasting must be thought of in that setting. The talks and addresses reprinted in this book represent two weekly broadcasts—the "People's Service" and "Talking With You"—devised to meet the needs of the Light Programme. The "People's

Service" has largely abandoned the traditional form of church services. It does not assume that the majority of people who are interested enough in religion to listen to a service are still quite familiar with Christian language and Christian ideas. Without attempting in any way to water down Christian truth, it tries to begin where people are, and to build up the service from that point. The attempt has been justified not only by the audience of three and a half millions that listens every Sunday, but also by the quality of such addresses as those given by Dr. Soper. "Talking With You" is an attempt to bring together a Christian who has something to say and the listener who is in the mood for a man who will talk *with* him, but not for a man who insists on talking *at* him. Despite obvious limitations and the vast audience, broadcasting can be a surprisingly intimate affair in the hands of a good broadcaster. How well Dr. Soper has succeeded—in the very difficult period of five minutes—will be known by those who have heard him.

It is obviously not my business in an introduction to appraise what this book contains, or to express my opinion about this or that statement. What I can do, from some experience of broadcasting, is to draw attention to the way it was presented on the air. Three points stand out very clearly in the "People's Service" addresses. (a) Dr. Soper begins where people are and then proceeds by the logic of people's experiences.

He does not allow himself to be tied down by an academic scheme, but is led from one point to another by what happens in people's lives. That method makes it possible for people to respond to what he says. (b) Although the services were not "traditional" they were *shapely* and they had movement. Each service was an act of worship with a definite goal and moved steadily towards it. (c) Dr. Soper concentrates on essentials. There is no waste, no irrelevance. Every illustration builds up the whole.

The second series of talks—based on long experience in the open air—shew very clearly the merit of beginning where people are. Note too how in the first series the speaker gave five talks "putting Christianity on the map to-day" before he felt himself free to deal with some fundamental facts of the Christian life. And all the while he does not disguise what he is talking about and aiming at.

No one can pretend that the task of communicating Christian truth to-day is an easy business. Here, at the very least, is a most effective beginning.

KENNETH GRAYSTON,
*Acting Director of Religious
Broadcasting, B.B.C.*

PART ONE

"TALKING WITH YOU"

I

BEGINNING AT THE RIGHT PLACE

I REMEMBER what put me off religion as a boy: two ways of talking about it which I'm sure were both bad and which I am sure have got nowhere. The first was to begin by talking about something else like gardening or snooker, and then suddenly, when the psychological moment had arrived, to pop in the bit about the "garden of the soul" and the "game of life". It's like those wretched short films which start off all right but just as the plot is hotting up nicely you find you've been had—it's an advertisement for toothpaste. Now I expect you have all had some of this and do not want any more. Well, as far as I am concerned you won't get it.

The second and even worse method was to apologize for religion—to give people the impression that it was jolly decent of them to take an interest, and in acknowledgement there wouldn't be too much said on the more serious and demanding side of it. In fact they would hardly know it was religion at all. I'm sure that's no

good. Don't you think people in their hearts
first despise and then ignore this mock modest
"if I may say so" attitude? I do.

Now I am a parson, and these talks with you
will be definitely about religion all the time. I
hope, to quote Gillie Potter, that I shall be
speaking to you in English, that is, in ordinary
everyday words and phrases—because you don't
read the Bible much (most of you don't read it
at all) and so you are not familiar with its
splendid but Elizabethan prose. I'll try not to
be dull and I will try to keep clear of patter and
padding, but I am certainly not going to apologize for the Christian faith, and I do not think it
good of you to take an interest in religion—I
think you are very foolish if you don't.

However badly I may be speaking about
Christianity, it is the good news that humanity
needs to hear and it is the only way of life that
will bring peace and security for everybody. I
am sure of that and so I am sure that you, and
I, and everybody else, have got to get together
inside the Church and outside it, to talk it out,
thrash it out and live it out. Why don't we? I
dare say there are a hundred reasons. I dare say
most of you have thought of some of them, so
let me tell you what I believe.

I believe that we've got religion mixed up
with so much misrepresentation, superstition,
"churchianity", and pep talks, that most of us
have lost touch with its real meaning altogether.
Religion is power, and power, according to

Bertrand Russell, is the "production of intended effects". It's so much more than fine ideas, pious noises, and good advice, that nobody can carry out—it's getting a move on in the right direction. In the simplest words, it's getting things done. I want to talk with you about this Christianity that gets things done that otherwise aren't done. If I can persuade you that Christianity means the difference between hoping for a better world and better people in it, including yourself, and actually getting this better world, then isn't that worth talking about?

II

THE GOSPEL IN THE PRESENT TENSE

I BEGAN to say that I believe it *is* really worth while talking together about Christianity because Christianity is the power to get things done—the things that badly want doing and are not being done. Christianity is practical politics now—it gets down to the brass tacks of to-day.

I wonder whether you remember a comedian named Milton Hayes? He used to recite what he called the meanderings of Monty—nothing to do with Field Marshals, but a kind of running, or rather stuttering, commentary on the affairs of the day. Many comedians since have copied

his incoherent style without acknowledging
where they got it from. I thought he was very
funny and often very shrewd. I heard him once
say, "Darwin tells us where we've come from
and Conan Doyle tells us where we're going to,
and if only the Prime Minister will tell us where
the dickens we are now, I'd buy him a new hat."
Now Christianity does tell us where we've come
from, whereas Darwin really only tells us what
we've been up to on the way, and Christianity
does tell us where we're going to—and I think
its information on the subject much more comprehensive than that of Conan Doyle—but above
all it tells us where we are now, how we stand
and how we can get going in the right direction.
That's real power and no amount of information
about the past or invitation to the future can
make up for the lack of it. Major Monday who
hasn't got past the Boer War is a joy in ITMA,
but he'd be a tragedy in real life—in fact he is,
because there are a lot of Major Mondays clutter-
ing up the place. We can and must learn from
the past but we can't either live in it or live by
it. History is a textbook not a dynamo—it
isn't the power we need to get on with the jobs
that have to be done.

And you can't live in the future either—that's
why so many of you are fed up with the religion
of "pie in the sky when you die". That sort of
thing is dope, not dynamite. This "Happy Land
far far away" (and incidentally, it's not only in
Churches that they sing about it—scientists and

materialists have been singing about it just as lustily, the only difference being that they've chosen another site for it)—this Happy Land is just too far away to make much difference to our lives now.

In a word we can't live on a diet of jam yesterday, jam to-morrow, but never jam to-day—wouldn't you trade all that unsatisfying jam for even "bread and scrape" now? All right then. Christianity is good news for to-day. It interprets the past and opens up the future because it changes the present. When the Christian prays, "Give us *this* day our daily bread", that's exactly what he means—he is asking God to give us what we need to get going and to keep going to-day, and a bit over to get us started again to-morrow. And I'm not talking about spiritual loaves, but bread that starving millions are crying out for all over the world. There's nothing so urgent as hunger, hunger won't wait. It's no good telling a hungry man to take the long view. Nothing is practical politics that doesn't face this urgent and immediate need for bread. Christianity is practical politics because it does. Every decent person would feed the starving if he could. Christianity says we can because in God's goodness there's always enough to go round. It will be all right if we share it now.

III

DIRECTIONS FOR USE

I WAS talking with you about Christianity as the power we can lay our hands on *now* to change the world and its affairs for the better and, my word, how it needs it! However, instead of bemoaning the situation in general I'd like to say something more in particular about this power of God.

If you think of religion as the medicine we all need to put us right and to keep us well, then it is medicine with directions on the bottle. A bottle of medicine may be just what the doctor ordered but if it has lost its label you don't know whether to take a drop or a basinful, whether to drink it or sniff it, or to rub it in, as the temperance advocate interpreted Paul's advice to "take a little wine for thy stomach's sake".

Now Christianity is power with directions for use, otherwise it's a medicine that doesn't get taken. I sallied out the other morning to do some gardening. There was no doubt that the garden needed doing, and, I would modestly add, there was no doubt about my good intentions to do it. I'd got the tools and I was ready for the work. I looked earnestly at the lawn, the desolation of the flower bed, the ramblers needing attention, the crazy path full of weeds, and wondered where to begin with so much to be done. I remained poised for action, but not acting, until someone near and dear to me broke the evil spell by saying, "Well, don't stand there looking helpless while you are making up your mind how to improve on Kew Gardens, do a bit of sweeping up." And the fact was that as I began to do a bit of sweeping up the other jobs seemed to fall into their right perspective and the garden began to look different.

I come across very few people who don't agree that things would be a jolly sight better everywhere if we all lived out the Sermon on the Mount. That's what wants doing in the world. I spend a fair amount of time preaching in the open air, talking about Christianity to anybody who cares to listen, and listening to those who have "a bone to pick" with Christianity, or, as it most often turns out, with the Church and with parsons in particular. Despite all their criticisms there's a remarkable unanimity that real Christianity is the spiritual and practical medicine we all need. Thank God for that. But it doesn't go far enough—in fact it stops short of action, and always will until that general feeling is jolted into dynamic action. It's like a motor car that has the engine and the petrol to take you where you want to go, but there's no self-starter or cranking handle so that you can't start it up. Christianity is a car with a self-starter to it, and a book of instructions. Now let's drop the metaphors. Here are the *Christian*

Instructions for setting about the job of making
the world the sort of place we already know it
ought to be. Take a look at Jesus Christ in the
New Testament, and at the saints of other
countries, past and present (there are quite a
number about to-day), take a look at yourself—
and it's not a bad idea to get some of your
family to help you—and then *compare the two*.
If you feel really sorry at the difference and
really sure that Christ is your ideal you've discovered the power to start up—in fact you have
started. And if there is anything "Better the
Day better the Deed", surely to-day, Easter
Day, is the best day of all.

IV

THE CHRISTIAN ORDER OF VALUES

DO you remember Noel Coward's production
at the London Coliseum, "One Damn Thing
After Another"? I believe it was a very good
show but as a definition of life I've often felt
that I wanted to quarrel with it. My trouble is
"Too Many Damn Things all at once". So many
tasks, so many claims, so many calls all pulling
at our coat-tails at the same time. You know
that stock figure in films, the harassed business
man with a fierce exterior and a heart of gold,
his table littered with papers, his ear to four

telephones while he endeavours to deal with his secretary, and his daughter, and the hero asking for a rise, all together. I feel that I know him all too well.

Of course on the screen it all works out all right—he finally gets things into order, the important things are done and the unimportant or less important things get lined up for attention as well. But that's not what happens off the screen. Outside the world of the cinema the problems have got on top of us and the worst result is that we've lost our sense of proportion. We're not doing the first things first, we're putting the emphasis in the wrong place. There's something dreadfully wrong when poodle dogs and racehorses are pampered and cossetted while little children are ignored and neglected, when to say that a man drops his aitches or splits his infinitives is considered a more serious criticism than to say that he is a moral playboy or that he exploits his fellows. (You know— "he's no good—can't talk the King's English".) There's something dreadfully wrong when you can find people who seem to think that it's more important to tell children not to eat peas with a knife than to see that they get the peas in the first place, and, most tragic of all, when men lavish their courage and sacrifice in profusion in war-time, but seem to think that selfishness and indolence are good enough for peace-time.

It's all very difficult, I know, and merely realizing that all this is distorted and out of proportion isn't the same thing as possessing the power to put it right, and, let's be fair, religion hasn't always been a help.

In an ancient book of the law you'll find these two laws immediately following one another: "Thou shalt love thy neighbour as thyself" and then "A garment of two kinds of stuff mingled together shall not come upon thee", and nothing to indicate that loving your neighbour is infinitely more important than keeping clear of cotton-wool. Now it's just here that Christianity comes in and makes all the difference, for Christianity is a standard of values *plus* the good news that they will work. Or, to put it personally rather than abstractly, Jesus tells us what things must come first on the list, and what is more He goes on to say that if you do put these first things first you need not worry about the others, for they will look after themselves. God has made the world so that it will work that way. If you put little children first then poodle dogs will get on all right; if men will listen first of all for sincerity and worth in what their neighbours say it will improve our culture as well as our conduct, if we see to it that everybody gets the peas they need we can probably dispense with knives altogether. Above all, if we seek the Kingdom of God first all other things we need will be added to us. Christianity is the power to put first things first so that everything else can come out right.

V

THE CHRISTIAN PRIORITIES

I'M trying to persuade you that Christianity is a first priority for all people of practical goodwill, and not a kind of spiritual luxury for a few, that we shan't get a decent world until we put the Kingdom of God first and keep it there, and that it's everybody's responsibility to do something about it. At the same time I'm quite certain that it's just as important for us to know what not to do, as it is to know what we ought to be doing. Of course with so much to be done we need a multiplication of labour for "many hands make light work", but if it's going to be done properly we also need a division of labour, for "jack of all trades is master of none". It's a rule in our house that everybody lends a hand with the housework as there's such a lot of it and so few to do it—by the way if you *should* hear of a—but never mind. This rule works fairly well with us because I know my place— I've been told quite clearly what it is. I dry up, I clear up, I stoke up and apart from the occasional threat of promotion to wash up, that is where my usefulness begins and ends. Not so with our youngest daughter aged three. Her enthusiasm is much greater than mine, her energy cyclonic, and I should be deceiving you if I didn't add that she is a most remarkable child. She is more than willing to do everything, especially the cooking, but her *efforts* to do *everything* result in such indescribable chaos that you want to kiss her and shake her at the same time. To know what's your job and what isn't makes all the difference between the order which leads to progress and the confusion which prevents it, and of course in many things all you need is a bit of common sense mixed with humility. A parson friend of mine told me of a barber who was walking in the Lake District. He came to a gate with these two injunctions printed on it: "Use McDonald's Sheep Dip" and "Close this Gate". It would have been a very bad thing for his customers if the barber hadn't possessed the common sense to realize that he wasn't expected to obey both these instructions. Unfortunately in the wider world of social and international affairs it isn't so easy to know what instructions are meant for you and what aren't, and common sense can't tell you. In this dilemma some people become busybodies and interfere ineffectively everywhere, others get so browned off and bewildered that they do nothing anywhere. Here again I'm certain that Christianity can make all the difference. Jesus tells us that in fact we can know what to do and what to leave alone (and not be anxious about it either), because we know what God is doing. It's when you feel the whole job is on your shoulders that you feel you daren't leave anything to

chance, but when you know that God is a Father
and at work in his family now, and when you
realize that when we have lost control he hasn't
—then it's a very different story and one with
a chance of a happy ending. It's the confidence
that the job of putting things right is a partnership between God and us and not a solo effort
on our part which gives us the power to do our
bit with the talent we possess. We arc not called
on to put the whole world right, but to concentrate on that bit of the world where we live and
work and where God needs our help, and having
done that to leave the rest. We're not leaving
it to chance—we're leaving it in God's hands.

VI

GOOD NEWS, NOT GOOD ADVICE

IT'S as plain as daylight to me that Christians
have got to get together, patch up their
quarrels, and announce in plain straightforward
language what their programme is in general
and what their plans are in particular—but
that's by no means all. For even if the Church
declares and you agree with this laying out of
the work, so to speak—this plan of salvation, as
our fathers called it—it's still only a blue-print
of the new order and you can't eat or wear or
sleep in a blue-print. The vital question is, has

man got it in him to get to work on this blue-
print and produce the Kingdom of God from it?
Is Christianity good news as well as good
advice?

The other day I dug up some school drawings
I did years ago when they were deciding what
subjects I should take for matriculation. I was
advised at the time to drop drawing and to
concentrate on history. Looking at those drawings again I'm sure that was a wise decision—
there was no future in drawing for me (all the
same I think I'll hang on to them as with some
modern standards of art you never quite know
in these days). But seriously, I could never be a
great artist—I simply haven't got it in me.
You footballers and tennis players, you know
the member of your club who suffers from the
harmless delusion that he is a star afflicted with
permanent bad luck—he is always "off form"
and it's never "his day". The melancholy truth
is that what he calls his "off form" is actually
his real form—he's a rabbit and always will be.
No matter how hard he tries he'll produce no
inspiration, only perspiration. He hasn't got the
gift for it.

This gift for athletic prowess, for music, for
painting or poetry, is only given to a few and
even these few would never have become the
Stanley Matthews, the Tildens, the Bachs, the
Shakespeares and the Rembrandts unless they
had cherished and worked at this gift. But they
had something to work on which we haven't got.

So we not only hand it to them, we must also leave it to them to achieve those masterpieces which are quite beyond us. But what of the masterpiece that we call the ideal commonwealth, the classless society—peace on earth and goodwill among men? Have we got it in us to produce this work of art—have we a gift for peace and goodwill? If not, then all our fine words about democracy and all our high hopes for a friendly world are a hopeless farce.

The only answer to dictators and bosses and "herrenvolk" is that we won't have them, and we won't be pushed around by them, because we don't need them—we can do the job ourselves, thank you very much. Give the common people of all lands a chance, give them the tools of power: they'll finish the job that the tyrants have botched! Now that's all right from a soapbox but is it true, are you *sure* about it? I wanted a lot more convincing than I could get from politics and propaganda when I first began to think seriously about these things, and I found it, I found that assurance in Christianity. This is what Christianity says to me and to every one of you. We are children of God, we may be stupid, weak, and disobedient, we are, but there's something of God in the worst of us, whoever we are. Black, white, yellow, brown, good, bad, and indifferent, we've got the stamp of God upon us. Although we can deface that divine image, we never completely smash it and it's never too late to mend it. The Kingdom of

God *can* come, because as Jesus says we've got
it in us—God has put it there as a gift. We can
produce it as a masterpiece.

VII

DODGING THE ISSUE

TALKING about Christianity without saying anything about sin is rather like discussing gardening and not mentioning weeds, and
yet I come across plenty of people who will
discuss the problem of creation or the inspiration
of the Bible with tremendous gusto, but mention
sin and they're off, or they only stay long enough
to say "the trouble with you parsons is you're
always harping on sin—don't be such a lot of
weary willies". And this attitude is not only a
dislike for a pretty grim subject—it is the expression of one of the most marked characteristics
of the present age. The sense of, and sorrow for,
personal sin on which almost any preacher or
reformer could count in past centuries has
largely disappeared—you may be frightened of
a lot of things but are you really scared that your
sins will land you in Hellfire? I doubt it. You
may regard the Capitalist Class or Fascism or
the Communist Party as evil, but it's an abstract
impersonal sort of evil, isn't it, in which nobody
in particular is to blame? In fact you'll even

find people to-day who are prepared to argue
that sin doesn't exist at all—I met one of the
bright exponents of this teaching in Hyde Park
a year or so ago. I was arguing that before we
can expect the general state of the world to
improve there must be more saints and fewer
sinners—surely that's fair enough? But not for
him. He informed the crowd that I was just
confusing the issue—sin and sinners were nothing
more than convenient words used by the super-
stitious to conceal their ignorance, and apparently encouraged by the temporary hush that
followed this announcement he went on, "And
what is more, I've never committed a sin." I
understand that he was the only member of his
family present when he made this claim—but he
made it and quite seriously. You see where all
this leads—something *is* dreadfully wrong somewhere, there's no doubt about that, but if nobody's to blame, least of all yourself, if you
don't feel that you are in some way responsible,
if it's all going on as if you weren't there, then
it's no wonder that you become cynics—mentally
paralysed. You begin by pretending that the
broken jug really did jump out of your hand as
you were wiping it, that the apples which the
farmer found on your person when he found you
in his orchard really did drop off the trees into
your pocket, then you go on to persuade yourself that when you told that lie you couldn't
help it, and when you cheated your neighbour
your action was determined for you by an

economic law, and before you know where you
are you're talking that nonsense about "what
will be, will be" and "don't blame me, blame
the system". Now make no mistake, I'm not
defending the system—far from it. To tell ourselves that we're O.K., it's the system that's
wrong, is a piece of dangerous self-deceit.
Christianity brings us back with a jolt to
realities. It's message is simple and clear, it
doesn't spare our feelings but it does make sense.
Jesus says that there's absolutely nothing fundamentally wrong with the world except the hearts
and wills of men who should be obeying their
Heavenly Father but aren't. The key to all our
troubles is in personal relationships. The fault
isn't outside us at all, it's inside us; wars and
poverty and squalor are the ways in which *we*
have messed up a world meant to be, and fitted
out to be, a home for the family of God, and in
our best moments I think we all realize that this
is the truth. I don't know of anything that
would do us all more practical good than to say
to God, "I'm sorry, I've been passing the buck.
Help me to put myself right—then I'll help to
put the world right."

VIII

THE HARD WAY

I'VE got the idea that many of you who are outside the Christian Church and indifferent to its faith would have much more respect for what we have to say if we put our claims higher and not lower. The queer thing about all of us is that it's the *hard* things which we think worth doing. I had some friends who used to live in Yorkshire and last year they moved to London almost around the corner from us. You know, we saw much more of them when a meeting meant a long train journey than now, when it's only a tuppenny bus ride. After the grim experiences between the two world wars we now know, or I fervently hope that we do, the difference between peace-making and appeasement. Peace-making was the hard road along which we could have struggled to happiness and freedom, and I believe we would have tackled it if the challenge had been put high enough; appeasement was the "tuppenny bus ride" and in our hearts none of us believed the bus worth catching.

A Christian Gospel that doesn't claim that we can only get to the Kingdom of God the "hard way" isn't big enough to grip and to hold people —it may tickle our minds and feelings for the moment but it leaves us where we were—it hasn't the power to lift us out of ourselves. It reminds me all too forcibly of the fisherman who spent a day up the river and when he arrived back home at night his wife said, "Have you had a good day?" "Marvellous," he replied. "Did you catch any fish?" "Well, no, not exactly, but I influenced a great number." The only people who are any use in the building of the Kingdom of God are those who have been caught for God, those who are "in the bag" not those who have been taught about God and are only "in the mood". You may remember that when Jesus was enlisting men to build that Kingdom he told Peter that He would make him a Fisher of Men. Peter caught three thousand in one day—the first day of Pentecost—yet the history of the last 1900 years might almost be described as the story of the fish that got away, and I'm sure that one of the greatest reasons for the failure of the Church to capture men to-day is that we are not putting the price high enough, we're not using the power that is generated when the Christian life is offered as an "all out" commitment of ourselves.

The true power of Christianity is in the drastic challenge to "take up the Cross" and that challenge has been answered time and again by men and women who would never have responded to an anæmic invitation to get to Heaven on easy terms. You've heard the words "take up the Cross" many times—I wonder whether you've got hold of its meaning. The

trouble is that the word "cross", like that other
word "charity", has been so cheapened that
we've forgotten its terrible historic significance.
Haven't you heard someone say, "We've all got
our crosses to bear, haven't we? Mine is lumbago
—I'm a positive martyr to it." Now lumbago
is bad enough in all conscience but compared
with true cross-bearing it's a mere fleabite. The
people who heard Jesus say, "Take up your
cross for that's the only way to my Kingdom"—
they knew what he meant. A man bearing a
cross was a man condemned to death, and he
was carrying two great pieces of wood to the
place where he would be strung up on them to
die. Taking up the cross meant looking death
in the face, for it was a man's final act—there
was nothing more that could be demanded of
him. He had gone the limit. Those are still
God's terms for the would-be Christian—to look
even death in the face for Christ's sake and to
go to the limit for His Kingdom.

IX

REVOLUTIONARY CHRISTIANITY

I WAS saying that being a Christian is a much
more serious business than taking on a few
more amiable habits and voting for a better
world. It's an "all out" revolutionary change

in individuals that leads to revolutionary mass action in society, and if anybody tells you anything less than that in the name of Jesus, don't believe them. Surely, no one thinks any longer that a fresh coat of paint will make the world as good as new. Western civilization in particular is past patching up—it always was, and in my experience nothing exasperates sensible folk so much as to assure them that things will be all right if we "make do and mend"—they need remaking not mending. I remember the first time I went to camp as a very tenderfoot in the Scouts. I was issued with a palliasse and four blankets and told to get a good night's sleep. In my innocence I laid the blankets gently on the palliasse, crawled under them and closed my eyes—but not for long. I found those blankets had a lot in common with the tow rope in "Three Men in a Boat" (you know the one that seemed to tie itself into knots of its own accord), every movement uncovered more of my miserable body, the more I tugged and pulled to improve my unhappy lot the more like a bundle of old clothes the bed became. At long last I gave up the struggle—there was nothing for it but to get up, and to start all over again. I woke a sleeping patrol-leader and with his disgruntled help we made the bed *again*, properly, from the start, and then I got some sleep. The human family has made its bed wrongly and that's why we're all lying on it so uneasily and wakefully. Until we get up and *remake* it properly *we* shall have no rest. Christianity is out to *remake* the world by remaking enough people to do the job. The Roman Empire wasn't left long in doubt about that. When the apostles moved in on Salonika, the local inhabitants said with alarm, "Those who have turned the world upside down have arrived." I wish to goodness that when the Church Assembly or the Methodist Conference meets this year people would feel "We'd better keep an eye on those fellows—they're out to start a revolution." The early Christians were known as the "people of the way" because the most obvious thing about them was that they were living an entirely new kind of life. They weren't just travelling more quickly, or more peacefully, or more confidently along one of the roads that led to Rome—they simply weren't on that road at all—they'd found a brand new road and it was leading them to another city altogether. If you've once made up your mind about the place you want to get to there's nothing so completely wrong as the road that leads somewhere else, and if you've been foolish enough to start walking on that wrong road you don't improve the situation by starting to run, you've got to get back to the place where you began and start off again, in a new way, in a new direction. That's how Christians to-day have to look at the set-up of affairs—just as Jesus said that the open secret of personal power is the moral revolution which he called "taking up the cross", so the open secret of freedom and happiness in the world is the social revolution called the "way of the cross". Obviously I can't describe the revolution in the minute I've got left, or indeed in a thousand minutes, but I can tell you how we can all start out together to understand it and to put it into operation. Really get to know what Jesus said about His Kingdom where love is power, peace is undivisible, and real brotherhood becomes practical politics, and get to know how He lived it out—and the Christian Church is still the best place in which to find out all this—then up the revolution.

x

THE REALISM OF LOVE

SUPPOSING you agree with what I have been saying about the need for a *new* and not a *patched up* world, and even supposing that you are prepared to agree that Christianity might be the revolutionary power with which to get that new world, most of you don't think much of our chances, do you? I'm sure you don't—and I'm pretty sure of the season too.

I'll try to put it in your way. You find Christians condemning violence, or I hope to God you do, as the power with which to get a new order of society, you hear them say that Jesus rejected power politics as a means of

achieving His Kingdom, and when you ask them
what they are going to *use* in place of atomic
bombs or armies or political or economic
sanctions to get their revolution under way they
say "love", and you feel you've been caught—
you've been looking for a fight and it has turned
out to be a game of "kiss in the ring". If love
were just "kiss in the ring" I should share your
exasperation, for atomic bombs and armies and
tyrannies do get things done even if they are
the wrong things, but telling the members of
the Peace Conference to kiss and make friends
is just fatuous—(just look at some of them).

Now I do most fervently believe that the
Christian Revolution means loving your enemy
into friendship, and loving your neighbour into
fellowship, that it stakes everything on *love* as
being able to make the world go round the right
way, but I hope I realize that we've got to
explain this love in terms of *power* and rescue it
from the rubbish with which it has got mixed
up in men's minds.

I won't waste much time with those who
having read the first ten pages of a fifth-rate
book on materialism have persuaded themselves
that love simply doesn't exist—though there are
quite a few of them about. I was talking on
Tower Hill some time ago about loving your
neighbour with all your heart and a heckler
interrupted to ask me why I hadn't given up
those silly habits about love—how could you
love with all your heart? The heart was just a

pump, that's all. Now I ask you, fancy propos-
ing to your girl and saying, "My darling, will
you be mine? I love you with all my pump."

No, our main business is with those who've
got the *wrong* idea of love and it wouldn't be
surprising if we *all* had considering the caricatures of the real thing that confront us in the
cinema and the cheap novel every day. If love
were the state that Betty Grable or Ray Milland
fall into in every new general release, then it
couldn't run a whelkstall let alone a revolution
—it's just a muzzy sentimentality at best, and
it's often not even as innocent as that. If love
were that "indefinable something" that fills the
pages of some novels, a pang, an aura, an "I
don't know what, but I want to bite her" sort
of feeling—you know the stuff—then no wonder
it doesn't commend itself to you as a weapon
with which to fight privilege and vested interest.
And, *more seriously*, if love were just a feeling
of affection for, or liking for, something or someone, as when people say, "I adore strawberries"
or "I'm very fond of George", it certainly
wouldn't provide the drive needed for a revolution. But believe me that's *not* the love that
you'll find if you look at the New Testament and
especially at Jesus Christ. Love for the Christian
is not a feeling *about* other people but an activity
towards other people—it's *action* all the time—
it's good will on fire—it's saying to yourself,
"I'll believe that the other fellow is my brother
even though he's my enemy, and I'll treat him

as a brother even though I don't like the look of him." It's the power of Jesus Christ who didn't *fall* for you and me but *gave* Himself for you and me. That's love.

XI

PRIDE—THE ORIGINAL SIN

YOU remember the old chestnut about the preacher who was conducting a service at a mental hospital? He was given to rhetorical questions and began his sermon by asking, "My friends, why are we all here?" and someone at the back told him—"Because we're not all there." I wonder how many of you have got the notion that churchgoing and religious activities generally are for people who aren't "all there", people who are amiable and decent and harmless enough, but not quite up to scratch or they wouldn't be wasting their time singing hymns and saying prayers when they might be out in the world getting on with things. Now I'm prepared to grant you that there are some "dim-wits" in the church, I'm even prepared to admit that you'll find a few in the ministry, but I won't have it that Christians as a whole are feeble minded as compared with the rest of the community. On the contrary I'm quite satisfied that if a true balance sheet could be produced it would show that both now and in the past the keenest minds have been found inside the ranks of Christianity and not outside. As an example, it seems to me at the moment that it's the Christians, rather than the politicians, or the scientists, or the lawyers, who have been alert to seize upon the inner significance of the *atomic bomb*.

No! the difference between the Christian and the non-Christian isn't that the one is "all there" and the other isn't—the fact is we're none of us "all there" and the Christian knows it whereas the other fellow doesn't, and *that*'s why the Christian says his prayers and sings his hymns. It's the childish idea of self-sufficiency that we all need to outgrow. Wasn't it Mark Twain who hit off this cocksureness to a "T"? He said that when he was a boy of fourteen he was appalled to discover how ignorant his father was, but when he got to be twenty-one he was surprised to find how much knowledge the old boy had picked up in the meantime. The real trouble with "cocksureness" is not so much that it makes you difficult to get on with, but that pretty soon it makes it impossible for you to get on at all. It's not only a moral disease, but a disease in which one of the symptoms is the delusion that there's nothing wrong with you, so that instead of going and getting treatment you tend to become a chronic invalid yourself and a centre of infection for other people.

The Christian Church has never been in any

doubt that self-sufficiency, cocksureness, or pride, as it most frequently has called it, is the deadliest of all sins, for it is pride that goes before the fall; pride is the original sin from which all the others descend because it is the sin which blinds a man to his need for God and so shuts him off from the wisdom and power of God. We're not all there and never shall be until God is there with us. It may be a blow to our pride to acknowledge that we need help from outside ourselves if we are going to grasp with both hands the blessings of peace and security which as yet we've only touched with our fingertips, so to speak, but pride's a high horse that won't go and isn't worth keeping. It's only when we come down off it that we find the power to get moving in the right direction.

Nothing that I've tried to say in all these talks will make any effective difference unless I can persuade you that you're in a *bad way*. Only when you realize that grim fact will you be likely to do anything about it. For it's only the man who knows his own weakness who finds God's power—swallowing your pride is unpleasant medicine to take but it works. I can recommend it—it's curing me.

XII

COME TO CHURCH

I WANT to put in a plea for the Church. I know that very few of you go to church at all, or at most on three occasions—christenings, weddings, and funerals. As a lady from the Old Kent Road once said to me, she liked to be "done proper", but even on these occasions you are more or less unconscious of what's going on especially if you are the principal parties at the ceremony.

What is the real reason why you have no use for the Church? Because, you know, the reasons you give when you are buttonholed about it aren't very impressive, in fact they are not generally reasons at all, they are much more like excuses. Here's the man who wouldn't touch the Church with a barge-pole because he says it's a capitalist ramp, but I don't notice him staying away from the pictures or the dogs on that account. Here's another who says he can't put up with all the "mumbo jumbo" that goes on in church so he stays at home and listens to "Chickery Chick Trala Trala". I've more sympathy for the man who says it's the parsons who put him off, because as a parson I know how congregations can put us parsons off—but it's the saints who made up the Church not the parsons as such, and there isn't a single church in the wide world that hasn't got at least one saint in it if you look for him. But of all these alleged reasons by far the most popular is the complaint that the church is so terribly dull and churchgoing such a meaningless waste of time.

Now it's quite clear to me that all this actually misses the mark, for quite apart from the fact that a lot of it isn't true, I believe that where these complaints are true they are sound reasons for getting into the Church and revolutionizing it and not staying outside and ignoring it, for as they stand they beg the whole question because they are based on an entirely false idea of its true meaning. For instance there are many activities in life which are dull but are necessary all the same. There's nothing more dull than travelling through Manchester or London in a tram, but if that's the only method of getting home then you take the tram, not for the ride but to get somewhere. Again, staying in bed when you feel all right may seem a meaningless waste of time, but if the doctor has prescribed a day in bed because it's the only way to get you really fit then it's the height of folly to get up and go for a walk. Don't you agree that what makes all the difference is whether the Church is *necessary* for us, and not just a pious club for those who like club life, or a form of entertainment like a cinema show, or a debating society?

If you and I sincerely want a Christian world

of peace and happiness we've *got* to do something about the Church because we can't have Christianity without the Church, any more than we can have a game of football without a football team. The mistake is to think of the Church as the football ground where the game is being played, whereas it is actually the *players in action* wherever that action is taking place. There's no such thing as a solitary Christianity —life is fellowship and the Christian life *is* the Christian fellowship. If you don't think much of that fellowship as you have found it, help us to improve it—all of you who are keen to see the Kingdom of God come, so that our children shall enjoy that full and free life that God planned for us all. Let us get together in humility and mutual understanding and tolerance to seek God's power and to do God's will. That's the true Christian fellowship. To be in that fellowship is to be in church. They are probably trying to do that in a church just round the corner from you, and they need your help.

XIII

PRAYER AS POWER

FOR the last twelve Sunday evenings I have been trying in a total of about fifty-four minutes to talk with you about the largest, and in my conviction the most vital, theme in the world. Fifty-four minutes is no time at all in which to *present the case* for even a single Christian doctrine, but it's quite enough time in which to have persuaded *you* to do something about that case for them all. I very much hope that I have. Thank you for your letters, especially perhaps for the critical ones. I hope that you have received a reply to all those which indicated where they came from. Let me say a word to those of you who haven't given me the opportunity to write back. One such correspondent confined himself to the single word "Bunk!" while another expressed the hope that I might be made to do an "honest day's work sometime", but most of them helped to confirm me in what I believe is a significant and hopeful sign of the times—that though there is a widespread apathy towards Christianity as a way of life, there is a widespread interest in religious matters as subjects for intelligent study.

So let me end these talks with a word about bridging that gulf, for that's what I'm really concerned about. How precisely does a man or woman who is interested in the proposition that Christianity is the power to get the right things done begin to lay hold of that power and to do them? Here Christians of every denomination have spoken with one voice. *Prayer* is the immediate technique of power. Praying is the pipeline along which the Grace of God flows from Him to you. Now I well realize that it's all very

well for the Church to say this, but so many of
you feel that either prayer is some mysterious
activity for a few peculiar people and you can't
make head or tail of it, or else if you think that
you understand what it is, you are just as sure
that it doesn't do what it says. And so you
simply don't pray. Now there may be a hundred
explanations as to why you think like this about
prayer, but I want to concentrate on one of
them and I shouldn't be surprised if it's the
most common. You are thinking of prayer as
the power to get what you want, instead of the
power to do what God wants—trying to get God
on your side rather than trying to get yourself
on God's side. Wasn't it Dr. Inge who says that
he once received a letter which said "Dear Sir:
You are a menace. I have prayed for your
death.—P.S.: I have been very successful in two
or three previous cases." Of course, you say,
that's absurd, but in principle it's no more
absurd than asking God to give you the prize
in a competition for which you have entered, or
even good weather on your holiday, and then
when you come bottom, or have it rain all the
time, assert that God hasn't answered your
prayer, and give up praying as a bad job.
Incidentally this attitude always prevents you
from seeing the simple truth, that God may have
answered your petition by saying "no" to it.
I'm not for one moment saying that you can't
tell God how much you'd like that prize, in fact
the more you try to talk to God as a loving and

understanding Father, the more perfectly will you be praying.

The point is that true prayer is the power to change you, not to change God—to change your lives and circumstances, by changing your desires and motives so that you come to want what God wants for you. Jesus prayed the perfect prayer—"If it be possible let this cup (i.e. the suffering and shame of the cross) pass from me. Nevertheless Thy will be done." God didn't answer that prayer by letting Jesus off, but by enabling Him to go through with it. I wish you'd say a prayer like that now—I know it will be answered.

PART TWO

THE PEOPLE'S SERVICES

I

PREPARING FOR CHRISTMAS
(8th December)

I WANT to speak to you about getting ready for Christmas—because I believe it has been catching us unawares and taking us by surprise year after year. That's why, instead of becoming our standard of action and setting the tone for our everyday life, it's just a delightful brief interlude in which we take time off, so to speak, from the grim facts and bad habits all around us.

(That's the tragic side of the carol you'll soon be hearing on your doorstep, "Christmas comes but once a year". It does, more's the pity—it ought to come to stay.) And of course we all know, deep down, that things would be utterly different and infinitely better for everybody if the spirit of Christmas really did last for the three hundred and sixty-five days of every year —but how long does it last? It begins to get under way sometime on Christmas Eve, it's still going well on Boxing Day for most people but it's gone long before we take the paper chains down—four days at most out of the three hundred and sixty-five and what we do in those four days makes so little difference to what we do for the rest of the time.

Why doesn't it? I'm afraid the reason isn't difficult to find. We have turned Christmas into a holiday and forgotten that it's a birthday. You can't keep a birthday properly unless you prepare for it—you can't keep the birthday of Jesus properly unless you prepare to greet Him as the principal guest at His Party. Of course, in some respects we take very great care to get ready for Christmas. Weeks ago Christmas trees began to spring up in Oxford Street, shops are already full of tinsel and imitation holly and coloured paper; in the business world "shop early" is just another way of saying "Be prepared", and at home, if our home is anything to go by, preparations for Christmas are well under way—the lists of those entitled to receive presents are being made, plans for the pudding are being laid, and a conference has already met to decide who shall be invited to share the eating of it. Now, all this is right enough, but if it stops there we're like the man in the parable who hadn't taken the trouble to put his best clothes on for the feast to which he had been invited as a guest, and so because he hadn't *prepared himself* all the other preparations did him not the slightest good —the master of the feast kicked him out. You may think it a bit hard on him but that's not the point, the point is that it's true to life, isn't it? It's true of the world to-day—in one sense we've got everything ready for the Kingdom of God except ourselves and because we're not ready all the other preparations are wasted—in fact they become a menace rather than a blessing. You and I have got to give our minds and lives as a present to Jesus Christ just as we give our presents to one another, or it seems to me that sooner or later there won't be anybody left to give presents or to receive them; we've got to find the real answer to the question of what makes a pudding into a Christmas pudding (besides the extra currants and peel that we have saved up), for that's the only way to make sure that everybody was intended to have them and nobody was meant to go hungry. So I invite you to spend time now in getting yourself ready. I know where to begin. Christmas is first of all something about God, it begins, like everything else that is real, with God and not with ourselves. Do you remember the song of the Heavenly Host—if we had composed it we should probably have begun to sing "Peace on Earth, Goodwill among men," but those angels were a lot wiser—they began "Glory to God in the Highest", and then "Peace on Earth, Goodwill among men". In the words of the late Dr. Temple, the worst and most deadly sin, the original sin, is putting ourselves first, putting ourselves where only God has the right to be. Starting with ourselves I wouldn't give much for the chances of Peace on Earth, would you?

From *our* standpoint the future seems likely to be much the same as the past—that's why there are so many cynics about. It's only from God's standpoint that things will be different and Christmas starts with God's standpoint. Do you know the Magnificat? It's one of the great Christmas songs and it's all about God. It was the preparation of heart and mind and all that Mary, who was to be the Mother of Jesus, made for the very first Christmas Day, and Christians have been singing it ever since.

MAGNIFICAT

My soul doth magnify the Lord: and my spirit hath rejoiced in God my Saviour.

For He hath regarded: the lowliness of His hand-maiden.

For behold, from henceforth: all generations shall call me blessed.

For He that is mighty hath magnified me: and holy is His name.

And His mercy is on them that fear Him: throughout all generations.

He hath shewed strength with His arm: He hath scattered the proud in the imagination of their hearts.

He hath put down the mighty from their seat: and hath exalted the humble and meek.

He hath filled the hungry with good things: and the rich He hath sent empty away.

He remembering His mercy hath holpen His servant Israel: as He promised to our forefathers, Abraham and his seed, for ever.

Glory be to the Father, and to the Son: and to the
Holy Ghost;

As it was in the beginning, is now, and ever shall be:
world without end. Amen.

I wish all those who think that Christianity is
a mushy, vague, unintelligent superstition would
read it and listen to it and let its message lay
hold of them. Here are three facts among many
others about God in the Magnificat. It starts
with Mary's confidence that God is concerned
with us and has dealings with us as individuals.
He's not only the great architect of the universe
—(I never think that's much of a description of
God, anyway, though it seems to be a very
popular one)—he is personally in contact with
each one of us as His children: that's what
the theologians mean when they say that
Christianity is "through and through personal".

We can never think straight about religion
unless we begin with a God who is in touch with
us through His personality and ours, *rather* than
beginning with the idea of "laws which never
can be broken". God lives in His Family and
not in some cosmic laboratory. God is interested
in you and me and everybody else as individuals:
as Mary sang, "God has done great things for
me." Just as any little child always makes us
think of homes and parents, rather than of
equations and formulae, so the child of Bethlehem *makes* us think of God as the Heavenly
Father who loves each one of us. And it doesn't

stop there—the second fact is that the same God
who cares for us as individuals possesses the
power to achieve those loving purposes which
He has for His children. Mary sang "He hath
shewed *strength* with His arm" and then follow
those terrific words which make all other revolutionary manifestos sound about as exciting and
explosive as a recipe for batter-pudding. "He
hath put down the mighty from their seats and
hath exalted the humble and meek—He hath
filled the hungry with good things and the rich
He hath sent empty away." Don't you feel like
saying, "That's the stuff to give them"? Well,
be careful! for it's a dangerous emotion to enter-
tain, but if you really see what it means then
you can believe it with all your heart. Jesus,
born in a cattle shed among poor peasant folk,
is the hope of all the oppressed and downtrodden
people in the wide world. His Father and ours
cares for them and His power is available for
them—they will get justice—tyrants will be
overthrown, the rich will have a very salutary
taste of what it feels like to go without, "the
meek will inherit the earth". The universe is on
the side of righteousness and peace—for God is
at work for us and with us. The Christmas
message is the one authentic hope for the future.
One thing more: all this that we celebrate at
Christmas is no sudden fad and afterthought in
the mind of God—the birth of Jesus links yesterday, to-day, and to-morrow, together in the
eternal plan of God. God is saying to us at

Christmas time the same things "as He spake to our forefathers Abraham and His seed for ever". That's the great fact with which the Magnificat ends. Christmas doesn't contradict any other facts that honest men have discovered—it isn't a queer belief or occurrence unlike anything else that we know about—it's message is what God has always been saying to His children, but they couldn't fully understand it until at last it is made quite clear in Jesus. You'll find it all there in Jesus Christ, just as Mary saw it all as she thought of the baby who was going to be born to her: God who cares for each of us and deals with us in love, God who is the fountain of justice and in whose power is the one hope of peace and goodwill on earth, and God who is the same yesterday, to-day and for ever, so that we can trust Him and depend upon Him at all times.

I suppose it's a fairly hard life for most people to-day. I'm sure it's a terrible life for some, but it's still God's world and God is at work, especially through Jesus Christ, so something can be done about it all if we can find God and get in touch with Him. The best way I know of finding God is getting to know about Jesus, and Christmas is the great time to do it. It will lift your heart up, it will turn your eyes to the future with faith and hope as it did for Julia Ward Howe when she wrote "Mine Eyes have seen the glory of the coming of the Lord".

II

WHAT CHRISTMAS HAS TO SAY ABOUT MAN
(15th December)

LAST week I was inviting you to get ready for Christmas by thinking of what Christmas has to say about God, for I'm sure that although most people don't seem to think it matters very much, in reality by far the most important fact in the universe is that God *is at work*—it is *because* God is at work for justice and peace that it's worth our while hoping that they will be realized. But that doesn't mean that all we have to do is to sit back and leave God to it. The theology of Christians has always taken the wrong turning when it has concentrated on God's power alone. The result has been seen in all kinds of caricatures of the Christian's life. Haven't you come across the man who spends all his time with his hat and coat on, so to speak, waiting for the end of this wretched world in which there's nothing he can do to put things right, or the woolly minded dreamer, whose head is always in the clouds and who never comes down to earth, or the preacher who wants us to believe that man is utterly depraved and helpless? They are all the victims of the fatal half-truth that we need God—of course we do, but it is not irreverent but absolutely accurate to say that God *also* needs us, and that's why those evangelical hymns about "leaving it all to the Lord" are a hindrance rather than a help.

Christmas is *first* a great declaration about God, what He is like and what He is doing, but it is also just as great a declaration about man. The incarnation, which is the theological word describing what happened in Bethlehem, is God's way of bringing these two great declarations together in Jesus Christ, who is the Son of God and the Son of Man. So Christmas not only gives to God the first place, but gives to man his right place in God's world, and whoever you are who may be listening at this moment you won't want to quarrel with the assertion that man in the modern world has *lost the place*—there's something fundamentally wrong when *man* becomes the pawn in the game of power politics, or a commodity to be bought and sold like coke by big business, or a guinea pig in the scientist's laboratory, or cannon fodder in the war machine, or the servant of the nation-state, or worst of all when he is "man the unknown" in a world where he seems to know almost everything else. No wonder that Bill Jones opens his morning newspaper, reads the headlines and feels that there's a terrible lot going on but it's all going on over his head. No wonder he feels that he is left out of account altogether and on the few occasions when he is invited to come into the picture it's the wrong picture. We are all in desperate need of a new doctrine of man—the ordinary "common or garden" man, and we can't afford to wait much longer for it, for all our dangers are not only larger to-day but *quicker*—that's what the man meant who said pithily, "Atomic power is here to stay; the important question is, are we?" It's all very well to know what we were like thousands of years ago, it's all very well to be told what we shall be like in the glorious future—what we want to know is the truth about ourselves now. Are we all competent beings temporarily paralysed by lack of education, are we just another species like the ant destined to end up in a sort of totalitarian ant-heap, are we totally depraved sinners dependent entirely upon the inscrutable mercy of God, are we on the way out of a universe which is cooling off, or on the way in to an earthly paradise the secret of which is held by the economist? I've heard all these suggestions and many more made in Hyde Park, sometimes by people who have thought about these things deeply, often by people whose attitude is that any answer is better than none. What do you think?

I'm quite certain that many of you find it all so complicated and bewildering that instead of finding an answer which gets you on to your feet, you've got the sort of headache which is tending to lay us *all* out, and keep us off work and off our food. Now I do fervently believe that the message of Christmas is not an aspirin for this headache—it's the cure for it. The birth of Jesus is not a fairy story about imaginary people living in a world of fancy—it is a piece of hard fact, a piece of history if you like, which gives us the key to the meaning of ourselves in God's world. It really does put us in our place, gives us our bearings and our marching orders. You may remember that last Sunday we used as an illustration of what Christmas has to say about God, the Magnificat, the song that Mary sang in His praise and in recognition of His love and power. There's another great Christmas song— it's called the Benedictus. It is ascribed to Zacharias, the father of John the Baptist—John the Baptist who was Jesus's cousin and had a most important part to play in preparing the way for Jesus. Zacharias had caught the vision of our human share in God's purposes—and the Benedictus, after speaking about God, brings *men* like David and Abraham, the fathers and the prophets of Israel, and especially John himself, into the Christmas picture. I believe if you read with imagination you will find not only God's name but *yours* in the Benedictus.

BENEDICTUS

BLESSED be the Lord God of Israel: for He hath visited, and redeemed His people;

And hath raised up a mighty salvation for us: in the house of His servant David;

As He spake by the mouth of His holy Prophets: which have been since the world began;

That we should be saved from our enemies: and from the hands of all that hate us;

To perform the mercy promised to our forefathers: and to remember His holy Covenant;

To perform the oath which He sware to our forefather Abraham: that He would give us;

That we being delivered out of the hand of our enemies: might serve Him without fear;

In holiness and righteousness before Him: all the days of our life.

And Thou, Child, shalt be called the Prophet of the Highest: for Thou shalt go before the face of the Lord to prepare His ways;

To give knowledge of salvation unto His people: for the remission of their sins,

Through the tender mercy of our God: whereby the day-spring from on high hath visited us;

To give light to them that sit in darkness, and in the shadow of death: and to guide our feet into the way of peace.

Glory be to the Father, and to the Son: and to the Holy Ghost;

As it was in the beginning, is now, and ever shall be: world without end. Amen.

If the Magnificat is the Manifesto of the Kingdom of God then the Benedictus is like the programme of the Kingdom. I'll suggest to you three things it says about us in that programme. First it says that man is the servant of God like David was, and his destiny on earth is "to serve Him in holiness and righteousness

all the days of our life". If man is to be the
master of his circumstances and the master of
himself he can only do so by becoming the
servant of God. We don't like the word "servant" and it's not surprising, for the word has
become degraded, but in our revolt against
"servitude" we tend to talk a great deal of nonsense about freedom. True freedom isn't taking
orders from nobody but taking orders from the
right person. James Ward said, "the only
freedom worth having is the freedom to do God's
will," for God's service is perfect freedom. The
lack of this "Divinely ordered restraint" lies
behind so much of the moral anarchism, particu-
larly among young people to-day—workshy,
irresponsible, irreverent—of course they are—
what else can you expect when they don't know
what their lives are for? Some form of discipline
and obedience to some kind of authority or
person is absolutely indispensable, and if it is
not given willingly to God that freedom will be
imposed upon us by tyrants, or it will be cor-
rupted by state or class or party. Obedience is
the key to man's happiness and his freedom.
That's why I ask you when you think about
Christmas to look at Jesus, whose name is above
every name because in the words of St. Paul "He
became obedient even unto death". I know of
nothing that can give such a sense of purpose
and worthwhileness to ordinary people than to
tell them that the job of living has not been left
on *their* hands—but God who made them has

laid out the work that they can do and ought to do, and if they will do their part obediently they can leave the rest in *His* hands.

Now a <u>second fact</u> about ourselves in the Benedictus. We are God's servants, not His slaves—our place in God's world is as obedient children who carry out our part with understanding, and not just as "moving instruments" (as Aristotle described slaves) whose obedience to God is mechanical and blind. Our job is like that of John the Baptist—"to go before the face of the Lord to prepare His Ways—to give knowledge of salvation unto His people". Putting that into the jargon of the twentieth century, man has the job of putting God's plan across in terms of politics and citizenship to-day so as to make it real and intelligible to others—for God has no voice with which to speak to the peoples of England and Russia and America and China and Germany and Japan, except our voice. We have to translate "peace on earth, goodwill among men" into bread and butter, and jobs and security, and we can if we try. *We* have to interpret the love of God to the persecuted and the outcast, to the bitter and the hateful, and that's not the job for a few specialists, or bishops, or parsons, it's the business of us all. If everybody already inside the Church would consider himself or herself called to be a witness to what God's purposes are, there would be a new wave of zeal and fervour in organized Christianity, and a new unity among Christians, but, better

even than that, poor despondent downtrodden
men and women all over the world would be
transformed by hearing the good news of God's
love and power in words they could understand,
and in ways in which they could share.

And so to the last thing I have time to say.
The Benedictus ends with the fact, above all
other facts, that with the birth of Jesus Christ
mankind finds its perfect expression—here is
man really taking his rightful place in the world,
here is man co-operating with God so that God's
light shines for all men in the darkness and in
the shadow of death, and their feet are guided
into the way of peace. Here is Jesus Christ "the
representative man", the Son of Man, as He
called Himself, who says to us all, "Follow me."
That's not only a challenge, it's a promise—it
means that where He goes we can follow. A
worm can't follow an eagle, but we, ignorant,
weak, unreliable, men and women can follow
Jesus because though we behave like worms we
were meant to "mount up with wings as eagles",
that's our true nature. I think that most of us
are secretly ashamed of ourselves in this
twentieth century. We've blotted our copy-
book, because we've lost faith in ourselves. Jesus
came to Bethlehem that we may get it back.

If you want to do your bit for world peace
and world justice, then here is the truth about
yourself whoever you are: you were meant to
serve God, you were meant to be a partner with
God, you were meant to be a friend and follower

of Jesus Christ. "Rise Up O Men of God, have
done with lesser things."

III

PEACE BEGINS AT CHRISTMAS
(22nd December)

I WANT to wish you a Happy Christmas—and
if that wish comes true it will mean special
and distinctive bits of happiness for each of you.
A much-hoped-for present in your stocking, a
family party that goes off without a hitch, a
good long rest, the chance to see some football
or a play, a few precious hours with loved ones
who are usually far away from you. These are
some of the differing ways in which each of us
will find happiness, but wouldn't you agree that
it will be a Happy Christmas for *everyone* if they
can forget their worries for a day or so? Especially the biggest worry of all: what's going to
happen to us and to our children in this atomic
age—is it peace or is it war?—for there's little
point in finding the answer to all our other
anxieties if we can't find the answer to *war*. You
see this issue of peace or war is no longer the
most important problem for society, it's the *only*
one—it's all or nothing—war now is "total".
That's the devil of it, and the thought of war
simply haunts everybody who has got a mind
to think with and somebody to love. So we are

looking forward to Christmas to take our minds off these things for a bit, though we realize that it will only be for a bit. We shall have to come back to them just as they were before. Well I do sincerely wish you that holiday from care, but I wish you more than that.

I want you to discover at Christmas time how to get rid of your haunting anxieties about the future, which is far better than time off from them. And you *can*! I know that is a terrific thing to say, especially to-day, and I only dare to say it because it is what God is saying in Jesus Christ. Christmas is the *promise* of peace on earth—the good news that it's *coming*, not the pious hope that it *ought* to come. Does anybody else dare to promise peace? Historians tell us that if the past is anything to go by there's not much chance; scientists hope so, but they are frightened to death by what they are doing; politicians are almost unanimous that though they want peace the only sensible assumption is that we must be prepared for war; the best that even many religious leaders can say is almost the same—hope for the best and prepare for the worst. And what does that universal figure, the man in the street, say about it? Very much what a friendly bus conductor said to me the other day—"Good luck to you, Reverend, but there always have been wars and there always will be." Of course there are thousands in every part of the world who see peace as a glorious ideal—who demand it in the name of common-sense, and who strive for it in the name of humanity, and they are the salt of the earth, but if you said to them, "Do you think peace is a foregone conclusion because the universe is on the side of peace?" their honest answer would be—"We don't know about that, but even if it's a forlorn hope we prefer to live and die in that hope than to go on existing without it."

Now, amid all these doubts and fears and "ifs and buts", I invite you to turn to Christianity and to hear the authentic ring of the Christmas Message—"God Rest you Merry, Gentlemen; let nothing you dismay". It's all right—Jesus Christ has come into the world to being peace on earth and goodwill among men—He is bringing it as God's gift to His children. That doesn't mean that it will just happen like a conjuring trick, there will be no magical influence which will suddenly turn gunpowder into soapflakes, atomic bombs won't disappear overnight, and warmongers and ruffians won't be transformed while they sleep by irresistible grace. No, somebody, you and I, will have to turn the swords into ploughshares and the spears into pruning hooks. But the glorious truth is that this job of peacemaking is the one we were intended to do, the world is the workshop already prepared for it, and, best of all, God will see to it that if we do our part He will be our guarantee against failure. In other words, Christmas turns peacemaking into "practical politics"—goodwill and realism become one and the same.

That's exactly how the first Christians thought about it, for when Jesus was born men were looking just as anxiously into the future as we are—for the Hebrew people the terrors of war were never very far away and all their prospects then and now are bound up with the prospects of peace. The Messiah who was to deliver them was to be the Prince of Peace, and so the Benedictus ends with the sublime confidence that Jesus will "guide our feet into the way of Peace". But perhaps the simplest and most beautiful of the expressions of confidence in the certainty of peace, now that Jesus has come, is to be found in the Nunc Dimittis, which is the third of those great Christmas songs which we have been singing in these services. It is ascribed to an old and saintly man named Simeon who had been looking all his life for the dawning of a new and tranquil day of peace for humanity and at long last had found more than a hope—a certainty. And having found it, he doesn't argue that it's a reasonable idea, he announces it with all the assurance of his heart. I'd like you to catch the infection of that heart-felt assurance of the Nunc Dimittis *now*— "Lord now lettest Thou Thy servant depart in peace".

NUNC DIMITTIS

LORD, now lettest Thou Thy servant depart in peace: according to Thy word.

For mine eyes have seen Thy salvation,

Which Thou hast prepared before the face of all people;

To be a light to lighten the Gentiles: and to be the glory of Thy people Israel.

Glory be to the Father, and to the Son: and to the Holy Ghost;

As it was in the beginning, is now, and ever shall be: world without end. Amen.

It's a relief to read about the future like that —it's so much more satisfying than whistling about it to keep your spirits up, and it's not just being carried away on the wings of a vague promise that "all will be well". The "Peace on Earth" that is God's Christmas gift to His world is a particular sort of peace—it has special characteristics. We can put it into words as well as keep it in our hearts. Let me put three things that Christianity says about peace into words so that you can make them your own and then pass them on to someone else. First, peace on earth comes through loyalty to a *person* rather than adherence to a *plan* or acceptance of an *idea*. Man is more than a political animal as they said in the nineteenth century and more than an *economic* one as many are still trying to say to-day, he is a *person*, and if you want him to respond to plans or ideas you must show him those plans or ideas in personal form and not merely on paper or in programmes. We know to our cost how a Hitler can move men to follow him to carry out evil plans, and to exploit false ideas, while the best plans and the finest ideas leave men cold and unresponsive when they are only to be found in pamphlets in classrooms. Ideas really haven't got legs at all until they get moving on your legs or on mine. Peace doesn't get moving until it comes alive in someone who explains it in himself and commends it by his life. That's what Simeon meant when he said, "For mine eyes have seen Thy Salvation." Jesus brings peace to life so that you can *see* it in action. Those of you who feel frustrated because your neighbours won't listen to your arguments about the stupidity of war, because everybody seems so helpless to stop the drift towards violence although everybody knows that the results are deadly, stop *arguing* for a bit and start *introducing* instead—introducing your neighbours to Jesus Christ, not as a theological figure, not even as the Son of God, but as the man who can make the idea of peace intelligible and real. I'm sure that it would be an excellent thing for us to stop telling the world what *we* think about Jesus and let *Him* tell the world through us what we are all waiting to hear—that man has it in him to be at peace with his brother man in the Kingdom of God.

Next, peace for the Christian is a universal thing—or in the popular phrase, "Peace is Indivisible". Simeon's confidence was world-wide and therefore complete. The salvation that he sees is something prepared "before the face of all peoples". Civilization has been paying a bitter price for this truth. The world has shrunk to the size of a neighbourhood, though not to its quality. We are thrown together anyhow, whether we embrace each other or smother each other. It was a tremendous step forward for a Hebrew to realize that peace for his own people could not come first in a series of similar blessings for other people—and that is the Christmas *step forward* for us all—there is no such thing as "one at a time please" in the programme of peace. Peace is a priority for all people. We can have peace for all now, we can't have peace for some now and for the rest later. That is God's will and nothing else will work. That's why I believe so much in the Christian Church despite all that can be said against it—it is the only world-wide community and therefore the one community through which world-wide peace can come. Let the Christian Church set its face absolutely against war and there will be no war. That's the road to Christian unity and peace on earth.

One more thing. Simeon in the 'Nunc Dimittis' did not forget he was a Hebrew and a *patriot,* but he saw what the real meaning of partiotism was. The glory of the "people of Israel" was not to be the glory of being a great power—of winning resounding victories on Rome, of dominating other peoples. The glory of Israel was that Jesus was born of the lineage of David, that from Bethlehem was to come the Prince of Peace and the Saviour of the world.

[handwritten margin notes: "Ghandi — how Neshu & Goa"]

[handwritten margin notes: "Jews & Eich- man"]

It is the problem of the nation with its prestige, its war capacity, its self-sufficiency, that we must solve, for it is the conflict between the nation-state and the world's need which is crippling peaceful planning everywhere now. Let me speak to myself as an Englishman— what is our true glory—a world empire, a great military prowess, a position of economic domination? No, our true glory has been in our poets like Shakespeare and our political institutions like the Mother of Parliaments. Our greatest glory could be as a Reconciler of the Nations— bridging the gaps between them by offering them the mediation that is free of selfish interests —becoming world missionaries for the Kingdom of God. All this can begin at Christmas time— let us pray about it.

IV

CHRISTMAS GREETINGS
(Christmas Day)

CHRISTMAS Day is the time for giving presents, and eating meals, and playing games, yes, and singing carols and praising God, but you probably think it's no time for giving sermons. I think so too—but if a sermon can be described as the "communication of a faith and the exhortation to accept it", then I suggest to you that there are very few, very few indeed, who won't do a bit of preaching, and eloquent preaching at that, before to-day is over. It's the job and the privilege of parsons like me to preach the Message of Christmas all the year round, but it's you who take over the Christian pulpits and wear the dog collars once a year at Christmas time, and to-day, in thousands of homes throughout the world, most unparsonic-looking preachers have already given out their text of "Goodwill towards men" and are expounding their theme, around the fire, in the kitchen, in hospital and prison, among the poor and the lonely. And what a hearing and a response they are getting! The world has suddenly become a different place—the greedy are giving presents, the workshy are hard at it, the cynics are bubbling over with enthusiasm, enemies are shaking hands, and coming to church this morning I nearly ran into a taxi and the driver smiled at me. It's nothing short of a revolution overnight, even the furniture seems different, and life itself is transformed. I wonder, have you realized that although we have become accustomed to this yearly phenomenon it really is a most extraordinary thing?

I try to imagine what sort of report a delegation from Mars would take back with them after spending the month of December on this planet. I'm sure it wouldn't be very complimentary, but among all the other queer and apparently

meaningless things they found us up to I'm sure
they would say that human things seem to live
two quite different sorts of life—one a life of fear
and violence and selfishness for most of the time
and then, once in a while, quite the opposite, a
life of comradeship, co-operation and goodwill,
and they would go on to say that when these
human beings were asked which of the two was
the *real* sort of life they said, "Oh, the second,
of course," and that was about the only thing
upon which they all seemed to agree.

That's true, isn't it? We find on Christmas
Day the one thing we've all agreed about—*this*
is the life, and our behaviour and attitude to one
another bear our witness to this truth. The way
we behave for three hundred and sixty-four days
of the year is only real in the sense that it is
actual—greediness happens, wars take place,
quarrels break out, but a Frenchman named
Edmond About once said a very wise word. He
said "There are many truer things than those
that have happened." There's another kind of
reality that isn't just history. Christmas is real
in the sense that it's right—it satisfies something
deep down in us. It strikes the right note, and
that's the only note that will do. You know how
it feels when the pianist at your party gets into
trouble with "Good King Wenceslas". You are
prepared to put up with a permanent bass note,
but when he reaches the last note and can't find
it, the wrong notes are real enough, but if at last
after a process of elimination he gets the right

note it's the most real sound in the world, isn't it? The tension is over and everything is all right again. The Reality of Christmas is like that—we've found the note that is in harmony. We may not be able to sing the tune right through but we know it when we hear it and we know when it's played out of tune. I believe God put that tune into your head—otherwise it seems to me utterly impossible to explain how it got there. God has put something of Himself into all of us, and that's the only conceivable reason why we dare to believe that Christmas Day is more real than any other day. It's no mysterious accident, we are made for God, and we are restless until we find our rest in Him. The Christmas holiday is what it is because it was just a Christian Holy Day—it was what happened on the first Christmas morning that put these real thoughts into our minds, and these real feelings into our hearts, and if we want them to stay there for good we must link them up again more firmly than ever with what happened two thousand years ago, what happened once in Royal David's City, for although we have forgotten it, or ignored it, we would never have known what we were meant to be like except for the baby who was born in a cattle shed and whose Mother laid Him in a manger for His bed.

We would like you to sing that lovely carol with us. Some of you may have sung it many times already this Christmas, but you can't sing

it too often. Some of you perhaps dimly remember it from years past and haven't sung it
since you were children, and it will do you good
to sing it again.

"ONCE IN ROYAL DAVID'S CITY"

ONCE in royal David's city
   Stood a lowly cattle-shed,
Where a mother laid her baby
   In a manger for His bed
Mary was that mother mild,
Jesus Christ her little child.

He came down to earth from heaven
   Who is God and Lord of all,
And His shelter was a stable,
   And His cradle was a stall
With the poor, and mean, and lowly
Lived on earth our Saviour holy.

And through all His wondrous childhood
   He would honour and obey,
Love, and watch the lowly maiden
   In whose gentle arms He lay.
Christian children all must be
Mild, obedient, good as He.

For He is our childhood's pattern:
   Day by day like us He grew;
He was little, weak, and helpless;
   Tears and smiles like us He knew;
And He feeleth for our sadness,
And He shareth in our gladness.

And our eyes at last shall see Him,
　Through His own redeeming love;
For that child so dear and gentle
　Is our Lord in heaven above;
And He leads His children on
To the place where He is gone.

Cecil Frances Alexander.

And now a Happy Christmas to you—a Happy Christmas to all *family* parties, reunited to-day perhaps for the first time for many years. Family life is the real way to live—we can be sure of that now because we can go to Bethlehem and see God coming into His world through the Holy Family, and so making every family a holy thing. The Kingdom of God will be built up from *families* not from classes or from nation-states or from "herrenvolk", for where two or three are gathered together by the ties of family there is God in the midst of them. Anything that helps to keep family life clean and whole-some is of God—purity, economic security, peace, simple pleasures, a house of your own— these are not just political or ethical objectives, they are Christian necessities, while war and poverty and impurity, industrialism and over-crowding, which tear the family apart and cor-rupt it are the great evils against which we have got to fight for our very lives. You've a grand chance on Christmas Day to recover something of the family spirit that we've all been losing of late years. Don't play the gramophone all the time, gather round the piano and sing the First

Nowell all together—play glames that everybody can join in—snap is much better than
bridge, and golf is thoroughly anti-social and
ought to be prohibited on Christmas Day. Even
if there are some gaps and vacant chairs around
the fire, close your ranks and don't let anyone
feel he's out in the cold, and I'm sure you'll
know something of "that peace which passes all
understanding".

A Happy Christmas to all children—this is
children's day par excellence. They come into
their own to-day. The child has his real and
rightful place in the world because Jesus Christ
our Lord was born as a little weak and helpless
child on Christmas Day. I remember, during
the war, that soldiers thousands of miles from
home, soldiers who never came to church all the
year round, would bring money and toys to us
here at Christmas time so that we could "give
the kids a treat". Christmas for them meant the
laughter and happiness of little children and if
they couldn't see happiness and laughter in the
faces of their own they wanted at least to make
sure that some other children were happy. The
hope of the future is to make the well-being and
happiness of children the first charge on our
statesmanship, and the test of our civilization,
just as we build up our programme for Christmas
Day, so that children will have as good a time
as we can possibly give them. When men asked
Jesus about the Kingdom of God He set a little
child in their midst and told them to look for

that Kingdom through the eyes of a child. The real world for all of us is where the little children of every country will have enough to eat, time to say their prayers, and not much to be afraid of if they hear a bang in the night. If we make a world like that, fit for little children to live in, the rest of us won't have much to complain about. Let us make sure that every child finds God's place for him in the world this Christmas Day and keeps it for His sake and for ours.

A Happy Christmas to everybody not forgetting the dog—yes, I mean that. Isn't this the one day when we believe that the world is one world and there's a place in it for all God's creatures? The spirit of friendliness to animals as well as the spirit of universal brotherhood is the Christmas spirit, and all because the cattle shed where Jesus was born is the one place in the whole world where not a single one of God's creatures is out of place. Look again at some of your Christmas cards, the real ones, I mean, not those counterfeit substitutes with pictures of battleships, or a fox hunt on them—look through the eyes of the great masters and see who have come to the stable to greet the baby Jesus: wise men, shepherds, Dutchmen in the Dutch paintings, Frenchmen in the French, Germans in the German—children, oxen, donkeys, horses, dogs, cats, birds. Listen to the carols about the Manger Throne—you'll find bird, beast and fish all represented as coming together there—there's even a carol about a monkey who found his way to Bethlehem. The real world is not the divided world, man against man, man against beast, or even creature against creature—the real world is the one in which Jesus is Lord of all living and in His love all creatures can dwell together in Peace.

And so "A Happy Christmas" to *you* because there's a place set for you, whoever you are, at the birthday party of Jesus Christ the Lord. Let us kneel for a minute there before we make merry in His honour.

THE LORD'S PRAYER

OUR Father, which art in heaven, Hallowed be thy Name. Thy kingdom come. Thy will be done in earth, As it is in heaven. Give us this day our daily bread. And forgive us our trespasses, As we forgive them that trespass against us. And lead us not into temptation; But deliver us from evil: For thine is the kingdom, The power, and the glory, For ever and ever. Amen.

V

THE YEAR THAT IS NEW
(29th December)

TO those who think of Christmas as something more than a holiday and the New Year as something more than a particular date on the calendar there is nothing accidental in

the fact that January 1st so quickly follows
December 25th. A really New Year is the con-
tinuation of Christmas and the coming one will
only be a New Year, in the sense of being really
different in quality from the old one, if we take
the spirit of Christmas with us into it. Leave
that spirit out of January 1st and you've nothing
left but twenty-four hours exactly like the 31st
December. That's the trouble with New Year
resolutions—they are made at the wrong time
and in the wrong spirit, and that's why they've
become almost a joke and have an expectation
of life of about a fortnight. Just before midnight
on New Year's Eve at parties which may be
decent and jolly enough but not conspicuously
Christian a great many people will be making
last minute resolutions to get up earlier, to cut
out some fault, to do a bit more for others, to
knock off smoking by so much (you can fill in
the particular resolutions out of your own experiences), as if there is some magic in the air
at that moment that will give immortality to
such resolutions. But far from being immortal
those resolutions are mostly still-born because
they come out of the old world of failure and
selfishness, which is the same old world whether
it happens to be New Year's Eve or New Year's
Day. There's nothing to keep them alive. They
need the environment and climate of a New
World to give them strength and enable them
to live. It's the New Year resolutions that you
make *to-day*, for instance, when the memories of

Christmas are still strong and bright, and its influences are still pervading our homes and our affairs, that have a real chance of survival. They will be born under ideal conditions, for the climate is just right for them. Christmas is the very air of unselfishness that good resolutions need to breathe if they are to thrive—I believe that they are almost bound to die in any other but that. There is *genuine* magic in the air that we breathe at Christmas. Let me quote you a typical example which I overheard as two people were discussing what they'd been doing on Christmas Day: "You ought to have seen Uncle George! He was twice the man he usually is— so good-tempered, so funny, such good fun— you'd hardly have known him." That's true of a lot more people besides Uncle George. That's how goodness *grows* in the right atmosphere. Let me give you another example. How many are there who, if you asked them in mid-July to sing a song at the children's concert, or to take part in some amateur theatricals would say—"Oh dear no, I couldn't possibly sing in public," or "I can't act"—but who are the selfsame people who have in fact been doing quite well with "Lily of Laguna" and giving quite goood performances in the family charades at their Christmas parties, surprising themselves and causing their friends to say—"I didn't know he had it in him"? He hadn't it in him in July, it needed Christmas to give it birth. It needs the spirit of Christmas to give birth to a New Year, and my word, how we need a New Year to bring back hope to the millions who in Central Europe and elsewhere are on the verge of the nihilism, of empty despair. Their condition is almost too horrible to contemplate—yesterday a nightmare, to-day a hell and to-morrow a hopeless void. We need a New Year to take fear out of the lives of whole communities who live from hand to mouth in insecurity and poverty; to heal the quarrels between races and creeds and classes, to bring joy to our unhappy, disordered humanity. Do you care about these things? I believe you do. Do you care about them enough to determine that you will *do* something? Then whoever you are I will invite you to make some New Year resolutions now. (Never mind the fact that you made some last year and they didn't last, never mind the sneers of those who will think you have "gone religious", and never mind if you don't know just at this moment what in the world to resolve about—don't *start* thinking about those resolutions from your end at all.) First of all turn your minds and hearts again to Bethlehem, because that's the place where we can find the wisdom to make the right resolutions and the power to carry them out.

I don't know of any better way of doing this than by singing, so we'll sing the old carol "See Amid the Winter's Snow"—it's Number One hundred and twenty-four in the Methodist Hymn Book.

"SEE AMID THE WINTER'S SNOW"

SEE, amid the winter's snow,
Born for us on earth below,
See, the Lamb of God appears,
Promised from eternal years.

> *Hail, thou ever-blessèd morn!*
> *Hail, redemption's happy dawn!*
> *Sing, through all Jerusalem:*
> *Christ is born in Bethlehem!*

Lo, within a manger lies
He who built the starry skies,
He who, throned in height sublime,
Sits amid the cherubim.

Say, ye holy shepherds, say
What your joyful news to-day;
Wherefore have ye left your sheep
On the lonely mountain steep?

As we watched at dead of night
Lo, we saw a wondrous light:
Angels, singing peace on earth,
Told us of the Saviour's birth.

Sacred Infant, all divine,
What a tender love was Thine,
Thus to come from highest bliss
Down to such a world as this!

Teach, O teach us, holy Child,
By Thy face so meek and mild,
Teach us to resemble Thee
In Thy sweet humility.

Edward Caswall.

And now *two* New Year resolutions and after each of them we'll say a prayer. I won't ask you to kneel or to adopt what is called the "Nonconformist crouch" or even to close your eyes, but I'm going to talk about Resolutions, not bright ideas. That means something decisive. I want you, if you will, to set your hand and heart to them in the presence of God—that's the reason for the prayers.

First *resolve* that you will get to know Jesus Christ. The key-word of Christianity is *"come"*, not *"believe"*. You can't make yourself believe in Jesus Christ, but you can resolve to get to know what He said and what was the meaning of His various actions. I have no right at all to say of you who have honest doubts about Christianity, "you ought to make a resolution that you'll throw them on one side, and surrender your mind to the claims of Jesus", but I can ask you to do what the shepherds and the wise men did long ago. They had plenty of doubts, but they made the journey to Bethlehem taking their doubts with them—it was only when they saw Jesus for themselves that their doubts turned to faith. *I* know that Jesus tells the truth about myself and everybody else, but *that* assurance springs not first from a resolution to *believe* what He says, but to *understand* what He says. It's a lamentable fact that a lot of people are much better acquainted with the ideas and doings of pugilists and film stars than with the one man who on any count has made

6

more difference to the world than anybody else who has ever lived. That's not so much a comment on their lack of religion, but on their lack of common sense. You *can* come to know Jesus Christ—he is no misty, unsubstantial myth. You can read about Him in the New Testament (in modern speech if the authorized version puts you off), you can come to know Him through the eyes of His friends who are called the saints, you can find out a lot about Him in the Church, and there's nothing wrong in going to church with no other intention than that. There are many fine and exciting books about Him—and you were not far from Him on Christmas Day. I'd be quite content to leave the verdict in your hands—I'm not afraid that men will reject the claims of a Jesus they really get to know. I'm only afraid of what will happen if He remains unknown. Let all of us who are prepared to make this resolution do it now and I'll try to say a prayer for us all.

COLLECT FOR NEW YEAR

The Circumcision of Christ

ALMIGHTY God, who madest thy blessed Son to be circumcised, and obedient to the law for man; Grant us the true Circumcision of the Spirit; that, our hearts, and all our members, being mortified from all worldly and carnal lusts, we may in all things obey thy blessed will; through the same thy Son Jesus Christ our Lord. Amen.

And the *second* resolution. Resolve that you
will keep in touch with Jesus Christ. Christianity
is contagious, you catch it rather than achieve
it. Find time to fill up your life with things that
are lovely rather than ugly, good and not bad,
uplifting and not degrading. Now that's a very
different thing from making a resolution that
you will *be* good, that *you* will get rid of the bad
in you—you don't get rid of the bad by *resolving*
to be good, but by spending your time in a good
environment so that the bad doesn't get a look
in. The best way for a man who has been drinking heavily to give it up, is not to make a resolution "never to touch the stuff again", but to
choose some amiable teetotallers as his friends
and to stick with them. As a prison chaplain I
know that though it's a good thing for a "lag"
to make up his mind to go straight it's a much
better thing for him to make up his mind to keep
away from his old associations and build up new
and better ones. You can choose your mental
and emotional company and that will make all
the difference to the kind of person you will be.
You can refuse to look for the *catch* in every
piece of good news, and the *snag* in every bright
prospect, and the *racket* in every human affair.
There's plenty of love and generosity, and down-
right goodness about and if you resolve to look
for these things, to think about them and to
dwell with them, you'll find that you really
want to be like that yourself—it's what is called
the expulsive power of a new affection, over-

coming evil with good, and it's what happened to those who came to Bethlehem. As men looked at Jesus impossible ideals became practical politics. As men stayed in His company they grew like Him, and goodness became His gift to them rather than their effort for Him. I believe that if you will resolve to practise the presence of Christ, to make friends with Him, filling up your heart with Christlike associations, you will find His Kingdom of Peace and Goodwill *springing* up in your own life and then you'll be free to work for it and win it in the world.

PART THREE

"TALKING WITH YOU"

I

FINDING COMMON GROUND

THE trouble with parsons like myself is that we have very little experience of talking with people like you who are mainly outside the Church, and at bottom the real reason isn't that we are a lot of stuffy bores, though some of us are, any more than the real reason is that you are a lot of flippant pagans, though again some of you are—the real reason is that we don't seem to have anything in common to-day, and you can't have a talk with somebody until you've found a conversational rendezvous. You may be an electrician and I may be a gardener, but if we're both concerned as to whether the Arsenal is going to stay in the First Division— then despite the fact that you aren't the least bit interested in seed potatoes and I couldn't care less about fuse wire, we have got something to talk about; there is at least a bit of common ground on which we can meet. Now I am a minister of religion and you are a wireless

licence holder—what have *we* got in common
that can become the basis of my talking with
you? Certainly not theology, at any rate in its
narrower sense, for although I find it fascinating,
yes, I really do, I'm also well aware that you
hardly ever give it a thought—it's part of the
strange world of bible-reading and church-going
and prayer-saying which is now only inhabited
by a small minority. There was until quite
recently a *theological* background to nearly
everybody's mind—and perhaps the greatest
revolution that has happened in the last two
hundred years is that this theological background has *disappeared*—so that you not only
stay away from church now but you don't even
know the name of the church you stay away
from. No, I'm interested in theology but you're
not, and it's not much use trying to get a conversation going on theology. Similarly, I confess
that I'm not in the least interested in some of
your concerns—I can't rake up the remotest
enthusiasm for the dogs. (Of course I don't
assume that all of you patronize them either,
but somebody spent over two hundred and
thirty million pounds last year at dog tracks.)
I don't know anything and don't want to know
anything about football pools, and I'd be very
quickly bored if you wanted to discuss film stars,
though I go to see good films whenever I can,
and I've got a soft spot for Ingrid Bergman.
We are out of touch with one another, and yet
I believe we can find a common meeting-place

and a common interest—in fact it already exists.
It is twenty years since I first started to speak
every Wednesday lunch hour at a place called
Tower Hill, which is a sort of "spouters' corner"
near the Tower of London. The crowds who
gathered there weren't interested in sermons or
anthems or religious pep talks, but I found that
they were only too ready to ask questions, and
especially to ask questions of a parson, so we
got together on that basis. I'd like to talk with
you about some of the actual questions that you
who are outside the Church do ask and which it
is our business as Christians to answer—or to
try to answer, for I'm making no claim that I
know all the answers. All I would claim after
twenty years is that I do know most of the
questions, and, what is just as important,
perhaps I've also discovered the sort of questions
that aren't asked. I remember when I started
I had prepared in advance some answers about
"justification by faith" and "predestination"
and "freewill"—I'd even got one ready on "Who
was Cain's wife?" but the first question I was
asked was about *Karl Marx* and I'd hardly
heard of him, and I'm still waiting for Cain's
wife to turn up. It's the questions that you do
in fact want answered that must be the common
ground on which we meet, not the questions
that you ought to ask. The Church, I'm afraid,
has often lain under the suspicion of being very
good at answering the questions that nobody is
asking; don't you agree that if organized

Christianity and modern society are to make
friends with one another, as once upon a time
the church and the medieval state did, the only
possible place at which to start is in this everyday world where we have both to face the everyday problems—where the Church has got to
justify its claim to answer those problems in the
light and power of Jesus Christ, and you outside
it have got to take these problems seriously
enough to be prepared to see them in a philo-
sophical and even religious background? That's
fair enough, isn't it? I'll promise to talk with
you each week about your questions as this or
that questioner has actually put them in an
open-air meeting, and try to say something of
what I believe the answers to be. Will you on
your side listen to the answers to what are after
all your questions, and if you disagree write to
me and say so and *I'll* reply either over the air
or through the post? One last word: I shall try
to persuade you on these Wednesday evenings
that real Christianity has got the answer to
every question, for I believe it from the bottom
of my heart.

II

CHRISTIANITY—WHAT'S THE POINT OF IT?

I WAS saying last week that if these five minutes are to be talking *with* you and not merely talking *to* you about religion we need to find common ground to start with, and that means finding subjects about which you are actually concerned to ask a parson questions, rather than subjects on which the parson thinks you ought to be interested. So let's begin with the question which in my experience crops up more often than any other—"What's the point of being religious at all?" Of course it isn't generally put as clearly or as shortly as that. Here are some of the ways in which I have heard it. "Mr. Speaker, you are always talking about religion as the way to get together for peace and a better world, but it's religion that keeps us apart—look at all the competing sects, look at the religious wars, and what about the speaker on the next platform who is denouncing you now?—religion is a hindrance, not a help—we'd be better off without it." Or there's the critic who says, "I'm looking for the cure for poverty and injustice—you Christians say you've got it but I find Christians in *every* political party, backing up *every* kind of programme, supporting all sorts of crazy schemes—officially you sit on the fence and I can't pin you parsons down to anything, and so I've no use for you or for Christianity." Again, in less censorious vein: "What can religion do that can't be done better by science and medicine and Parliament and psychology and good food?"; and, as one very rude young man said to me last week, "If I had my way I'd put you parsons to work instead of fiddling around wasting time."

Now, gentle listeners, I dare say you'll agree that as they stand these questions are somewhat too sweeping in their denunciations. I hope at least that you feel so about the last one for instance. There's nothing kills a conversation quite so stone dead as picking on the errors in the way the case has been put instead of trying to understand what that case really is. You don't answer an accusation by denying its exaggerations any more than somebody accused of stealing half-a-crown clears himself by pointing out that it was only two shillings; and I've no intention of getting out of the real problem behind this question by reminding you that Christians are not so disunited as some may think, or that on some great issues like gambling and sweated labour the Church has come down very definitely on the right side, or that ministers of religion do their whack of useful work.

All that doesn't alter the fact that we haven't made Christianity so *clear* and *real* and *vital* to people like you that you feel that despite all that can be said against organized religion you must be in it because it matters so supremely. If a car breaks down outside your house you might feel that it wasn't your concern if the driver was on his way to the "local", but you'd be really concerned to lend a hand if he was on his way to fetch the doctor for his wife who was ill. I'm quite certain that the right way to tackle this question is to try to persuade you that Christianity is out on the most vital errand, and that its breakdown, such as it is, is the very reason why you should come in and help. The great historic answer to the question, "What is the point of being religious?" is "To love God and to enjoy Him for ever". Perhaps a more familiar version of it, though not nearly such a comprehensive one, is "To save men's souls", but we'll put it into a completely non-theological form: the purpose of Christianity is to *make character*, and we who are trying to be Christians know that nothing else will do—our failures in the Church and our failures in the world are because we aren't *good* enough to live together and to make the best of the amazing opportunities all around us in the universe. We absolutely need a moral revolution if all the other revolutions in our thinking and our society are to be saved from ending in anarchy. You may be sure this is true of other people you know, but they are equally sure that it applies to you, and I'm certain that you are both telling the truth. Organized Christianity has made many mistakes, but real Christianity holds the key to character and because of that it's more important than anything else. Do you agree?

III

WHY THE CHURCH?

I WANT to go on with this question which so many people ask: "Why be religious at all?" I am convinced that the general answer is because religion is the natural character builder, just as food is the natural body builder, and it is impossible to be fit morally without daily faith as it is to be fit physically without daily bread, and, what is more, a world of men and women who are morally C3 is a world in which sooner or later everything else will be C3 as well.

Surely, put in this way, this isn't a dogma that the Christians are trying to ram down people's throats, it's a fact that anyone who takes the necessary trouble can see for himself? I come across plenty of people who won't *admit* it, but they always remind me of the man who thanked God he was an atheist—they denounce religion with all the moral fervour of minor prophets and they *actually* prove the very thing their words deny. No! man is born with a dog collar and he can't get it off—it's a permanent fixture and even when he is asking the question "Why be religious at all?" he really means,

"Why be religious in the way you Christians are?" This is how one listener has put it in a question sent to me: "Of course I agree about the need for religion. I've got my religion. I believe in Jesus Christ, the finest man who ever lived, and I try to keep the golden rule and do unto others as I want to be done by, but why all this Churchianity? Why all this religious set-up? That's what I say is unnecessary."

In the open air I find there's almost always a tail-piece tacked on to this most popular question by way of justification: "And in any case, Mr. Speaker, those outside the Church are every bit as good as those inside, if not a jolly sight better." I'd like to say a word about this tail piece first. I don't think much of it—if it's a complaint that Christians aren't as good as they ought to be, all right!—but as a comparative statement where's the real evidence—isn't it a generalization from a few selected instances? I mix with good, bad, and indifferent in both camps and my honest conviction is that in the matter of character the churchgoers have it by a comfortable majority, but I'd be glad to talk more about it with you later on if you feel that the facts are there to prove the opposite.

Meanwhile I'm sure the best way to tackle the main question is not by defending everything that organized religion is doing, that's impossible anyhow, but by trying to explain in ordinary language why Christianity, if it is going to make human beings honest and decent enough to put the world in order, demands a "set-up" and we can't be effectively religious without it. A good character is like a good education—you don't acquire it by saying you believe in it—you get it by going to *school,* and the Church is the school of the Christian character. Supposing we had been *talking* about education, would anybody want to say, "Of course I believe in the need for education but why all this educational set-up, why can't we have education without schools?"? I've no doubt this would appeal strongly to the younger members of your family, but it's a very good thing for them that you take a different view, isn't it? What organized Christianity is doing may look as unintelligible and meaningless to the outsider as a physics laboratory during a lesson might look to someone peering in through the window, but from the inside the meaning may be quite obvious because you know what it's all aimed at, and everything fits together to form a general pattern. Churches and parsons and Bibles and prayers and catechisms all fit together in a curriculum that has been worked out over the centuries to train men and women to make the best of themselves morally, just as schoolrooms and teachers and textbooks and examinations and homework play their part together in the realm of education. I grant that some churches, as schools of character, may be like Dotheboys Hall in *Nicholas Nickleby,* and some parsons may suggest a resemblance to Mr. Squeers, but that's

a powerful argument for better churches and
better parsons—it's no argument at all that we
would be better off with none, for where *are* we
to *learn* to play the game of life as Christians if
we "play truant" from the Christian *school* of
character? That's why I assure you that you
need the Church and the Church needs you.
What about it?

IV

THE CHURCH AND PRACTICAL POLITICS

THERE is one question that underlies many
of the letters I have received from listeners,
and it is also one that I am frequently asked at
my open-air meetings. It springs, I am sure,
from the bewilderment and frustration that
nearly everybody feels in the face of the modern-
world problems, and there's also a bit of irrita-
tion in it at the lighthearted way in which
Christians are prone to claim that they've got
all the answers.

It's this question about the Christian programme, or the lack of it. "Why don't the
Christians get together and give us a lead in
politics?" Now it's easy enough to ridicule all
this by reminding ourselves that the questioners
have generally made up their minds in advance

what that precise lead ought to be, from the enthusiast who wants the Church to throw in its lot with the Primrose League, to the zealot who urges us to back the claims of the Socialist Party of Great Britain. Some questioners go further still. They feel that they are the very people sufficiently qualified to run the Church on their lines; one man finished a long letter on behalf of a brand new political party after his own heart by saying, "Turn all the archbishops and politicians out—put me in charge and things will begin to happen"; I replied that I didn't doubt it. But there is something very real and very right in this demand for a united Christian programme, for the Gospel is much more than the good news of God's plans for the individual, it is good news for *society* as God's world-wide family, and even the friendliest of critics must contrast the precision and unity with which the various Churches have announced the plan of salvation for John Smith with the vagueness and disagreement with which they have set forth the plan of salvation for the whole society in which John Smith lives.

My own strong conviction is that the Church must declare with one united voice what the political principles are that belong to the Kingdom of God on earth, just as it has always declared inward principles that belong to the "redeemed soul". But I'm also equally convinced that the sort of programme that would emerge must be an infinitely higher and nobler one than any political creed that has yet appeared. It has always been a fatal mistake when organized Christianity has allied itself to even the finest political programmes—the Church can never be the "moral arm of the state" without debasing itself, and it can never *identify* itself with particular governmental theories without losing its freedom. If the Church attempts to run a political party the political party will very soon run the Church, like the man who tried to teach his pet octopus to play the bagpipes and it ended up with the bagpipes playing the octopus. The Church is much more like the House of Commons where there is not only His Majesty's Government, but also His Majesty's Opposition, than like a party conference where everyone belongs to one particular political colour—for it is the fellowship of *all* those who in the name of Jesus and by His power are pooling their resources and their disagreements in order to achieve a certain kind of world order which we call the Kingdom of Heaven.

Oh! I know it doesn't look much like that to some of you, and I am as disturbed as you may be at the absence of great political principles. If we only would declare them they could be the great rallying point of all people of goodwill who feel the need of a great spiritual dynamic to help us face the grim prospects in almost every sphere, so let me ease my soul by saying, as one Christian who claims neither infallibility nor saintliness, what I think this lead in politics

7

ought to be, and *will* be. I want the Christian Church, which, despite all that can be said against it, is the only universal thing in a divided humanity, to declare that just as there is this one fellowship for the world that breaks through all barriers of nations and class, so there can be one government for the whole world. I believe it's practical politics—I *know* it is! How I wish we could make this the centre of our thinking and the object of our preaching—to proclaim a new Christendom to which every man could dedicate his faith and his love, and his wisdom and his energies, every Christian saying, "We stand for one government for the whole world— that's our platform and nothing else will do." It's a colossal job but if you will help us to think it out and to act it out, it can be done because it is God's will. Isn't that the lead you want?

v

CHRISTIANITY AND THE COMMON TOUCH

IT is impossible for a parson to talk with people to-day about Christianity for very long and to ignore the rooted idea that so many of them have that Christianity is on the side of privilege and reaction and is no real friend to the working man.

Padre was an officer!

This is what is generally behind the questions which begin with "What about"—what about Bishops' salaries, what about ecclesiastical commissions and slum property, what about some reverend gentleman who has just died and left £50,000, and these questions are often decked out with those two standbys of the heckler, "Religion is the opium of the people", and "Jesus said, 'Slaves, obey your masters'."

I'll have something to say in a moment about the opium charge, but I'd like to polish off the other straightaway—Jesus said nothing of the sort, it was Paul, and he was no more inspired when he said that than when he told wives to obey their husbands. The real problem divested of all the extravagant and distorted accusations which so often go with it, and you and I know are easy enough to disprove, was put to me years ago at a huge left-wing demonstration which invaded Tower Hill while I was speaking to my usual crowd. We had a bit of a roughhouse, but finally, after we'd sorted ourselves out, the demonstrators agreed to let me speak for ten minutes as I'd got there first, and I agreed to give way to their speakers afterwards. When I'd finished a man shouted, "Why don't you come out of the Church—you ought to be on *our* side." He was sure, as some of you are, that Christianity was on the *wrong* side. He was a member of the great majority of human beings —the poor, exploited majority in every country and at all times who have never had a fair

chance in life, and he couldn't see what there
was in Christianity for him and the likes of him.
He didn't want charity, or promises about
Heaven or exhortations to be meek and patient,
he wanted someone to stand up for him, and
plead his just cause, and he had no confidence
that the Christian was the man to do it.

I'm afraid he is one of many, and so long as
this attitude prevails we mustn't be surprised
that despite the most cordial invitations,
promises of shorter sermons, tip-up seats,
special soloists, and no collection, the masses of
the people won't come back to church. More-
over it's no good just pointing to parsons who
are poor men in order to offset the argument
about the others who are wealthy, or to explain
that bishops' salaries aren't what they seem,
and their palaces are a burden rather than a
blessing. This is all part of the *defence of the
Church*, which, whether it is justifiable or not,
puts your backs up, doesn't it? In tackling a
problem like this where there is a deep-seated
feeling that Christianity is on the wrong side,
the man who leaps to the defence of the *Church*
may very easily win his case and lose his man.
Let me then try to answer him, not by an
argument about the Church but by an introduction to its Head. Do you know what was about
the first thing that struck people as they watched
to see what effect Jesus would have on the
crowds who listened to Him? It was that the
common people heard Him gladly. He, supremely,

had the common touch—He made friends with publicans and sinners, He chose His disciples from fishermen, He told the poor that the Kingdom of God was for *them*, and He said, "Call no man your Master, for one is your Master, even Christ, and all ye are brethren." What is more, the very reason why the religious leaders and the political "highups" were against Him was that He absolutely refused to take *their* side, and that's why they turned against Him and crucified Him—and that's why the first Christian Church which sprang up, just when they thought they had finished with Him, was a revolutionary mass movement of poor people who had found in Jesus their best friend as well as their Divine Leader. The plan of the Church in every country *to-day* is to proclaim the good news that the outcasts and the downtrodden, and the neglected nobodies, are the children of God, and each one is valuable in His sight, though not more valuable, than his more fortunate neighbours, and that the "brotherhood of man" and the "classless society" are *God's* ways and means to bring them justice and happiness. This is the real Christianity—of course there's much more to it than this, but this is the *practical* end of it—does it sound like opium, or isn't it more like dynamite?

VI

THE STRENGTH OF MEEKNESS

YOU'LL all have heard, I'm sure, the criticism of Christianity which begins: "We've
had Christianity for two thousand years and
look at the state of the world," and I expect you
know the answer reported to have been given
in Hyde Park to a heckler who made this
criticism—"Yes, and we've had water for two
million years and look at the state of your neck."
Of course in one sense this is a devastating
retort. The Christian graces and virtues have
to be kindled like a fire, they don't just happen
like the warmth of a summer day, and we've
had the fireplace and wood and the matches for
the Christian fire all the time, and if we're still
shivering with cold it's our fault for not lighting
the fire and keeping it burning. The truth is
that we've had the chance of Christianity for
two thousand years, but we haven't taken it
yet. But in all fairness to this repeated criticism
I must say that there is more to it than this.
Isn't it a rather clumsy and inaccurate way of
expressing the view that there is something
wrong with the Christian programme for changing the world, so that even if we did believe it
and act upon it, it still wouldn't work? There
must be many who agree with the listener who

put it like this to me: "I heard what you said last week about Jesus being on the side of the poor and advocating a social revolution to get peace and goodwill among men, but don't you think history has proved that the evils of society need something much more powerful than meekness to overcome them?" There have always been those who have contended that Christianity breeds the weak virtues instead of the strong ones; even that it advocates a slave morality, and some of you men who may be listening to me now have excused yourselves for not going to church by the monstrous impudence that Christianity is "all very well for the women and children". I'd like to talk with you a bit about this question.

The paradox at the heart of Christianity is that what we regard as the weak virtues are actually the strong ones—we've got our standards all wrong, and that's why we've got our affairs all wrong as well. A man who habitually carries a gun around with him and uses it, isn't likely to bother much about mastering the art of the "soft answer that turneth away wrath", because that very gun will give him a sense of security and will blind him to other and better methods of defence—until of course he comes across somebody with a larger gun, and even then he'll still be more likely to concentrate on bigger and better guns for himself than on the wisdom of throwing them all away. Human beings have become so accustomed to the sort of power that comes from carrying guns of one sort or another, that we have neglected the study of the other kinds of power. And *what* a state of affairs has all this produced—at the very time when science and culture are inviting us to enjoy the blessings of a world full of good things, we find that it is our "power politics" which instead of helping us to do so will destroy us—and we haven't confidence in any other sort of power to put in its place. It's like a man asked to play at a wedding and the only tune he knows is the "Dead March" from "Saul." Isn't it high time that we reconsidered our hasty verdict on the weakness of Christianity, as we call it? I believe that the love which gives, and often appears to give in, is in the end far stronger than the violence that tries to get, and in the end *begets*, more violence. I believe that the meek who are ready to obey God, though it means the "loss of face" and the end of prestige, are the only people who can possibly inherit the earth, and I dare to believe the greatest Christian paradox of all—that those who are ready to suffer for Jesus's sake are stronger than all the armies that have ever marched in His Name. These are some of the weak things which Jesus saw would "confound the mighty"—you can prove them for yourselves if you care to. I'll suggest somewhere to begin: Jesus said the best way to overcome your enemy is to "turn the other cheek". It doesn't sound right, does it? But why not try it?

VII

THE NEED FOR PURITANS

I WANT to say a bit more about the question of Christian morals, and in particular to try to answer those who think that Christianity will never work because it's "narrow minded"—that there's too much of "you mustn't do this and you mustn't do that" about it, and not enough "live and let live".

In my experience there's no criticism that makes such a quick appeal to the man in the street as this one, and no subject upon which the defender of the faith should tread more warily. If he isn't careful he'll find himself on the wrong foot, and his very earnestness will be his downfall. I remember one Sunday in Hyde Park I was arguing the need for temperance and a man asked me what right I had to condemn drinking when the Bible had nothing to say against it. I reminded him that, on the contrary, the Bible had some very definite things to say in condemnation of strong drink, and I proceeded to quote from the Book of Proverbs, with what I hoped would be impressive effect: "Look not upon the wine when it is red. At the last it biteth like a serpent and stingeth like an adder"—whereupon a man at the back of the crowd said he'd been looking for that sort of stuff for the last ten years. The crowd dissolved in happy merriment and the cause of temperance had temporarily to be abandoned. There's something very primitive and very right in the world's repudiation of a religion which appears to spend its time snooping around trying to prevent people from enjoying themselves, and I've no more use than you have for this negative sort of morality with its incessant emphasis on "Thou shalt not".

All the same it is true that Christianity is *narrow minded* in the sense that its mind is set on the "narrow way" which Jesus said leads to life, rather than the "broad way" that He said leads to destruction, and it does claim that "live and let live" is a universal ideal for the sake of which we *must* be prepared to say *no* to all sorts of things that we'd like to do as individuals. So let me suggest an answer to the listener who writes for himself and for many others, "Why are you Christians down on drinking and gambling—what harm does a drink do me, and why shouldn't I have a small flutter if I want to?" Well, speaking for myself as one would-be Christian, I should want to say to him, alcohol is no good to you even in small doses and is thoroughly bad for you in large ones; betting is a mug's game and an empty-headed waste of time; behind each drink and each bet is the sort of vested interest and big business which I've no time for at all, and drinking and betting in England to-day add up to two of the greatest social evils of our time. These are my convic-

tions, but not all parsons would agree with me,
but we *should* all agree on *one* answer to these
questions. We Christians are down on drinking
and gambling because we are realists. We know
that we shall only get to the Kingdom of God
on earth by the skin of our teeth and we need
every *ounce* of energy for the task of making
peace and building fellowship and maintaining
justice throughout the world. The dreadful mess
we're in now is the most solemn warning that
we can't have this Kingdom of God on easy
terms. It's no good kidding ourselves that life
is a sort of "happy-go-lucky sing-song" in a bar
parlour—it's much more like a fight against
almost overwhelming odds, or a race against
time, and we shan't win through because we're
"good sports" (a phrase which so often turns
out to mean "bad sportsmen") but only because
we are disciplined soldiers and trained athletes.
Christian morals are crisis-morals—character
training for critical times—and unless we can
say "no" to self-indulgence and this "happy-go-
lucky" attitude now, we shall not be morally fit
to say *yes* to peace and security in the future.
That's why no man can be a disciple of Jesus
Christ unless he denies himself—for otherwise he
won't be able to stand the pace. You footballers
are prepared to go into training for the sake of
your football team, you parents are ready to cut
out all sorts of pleasures so that your children
will have a better chance than you've had, and
it's worth it, isn't it? Then surely it's worth

while going into moral training and cutting out
beer and betting and many other personal
luxuries as well, when everything is at stake as
it is now. Has it ever struck you that what we
need is a Puritan Revival?

VIII

THE WAY TO CHRISTIAN UNITY

IF there's one single thing more than any other
that puts people off religion it's the scandal
of a divided Christian Church—don't you agree?
—and don't you think that the listener who has
sent in this question to me, hit the nail on the
head? He writes: "How can you expect us to
believe that you Christians have got the secret
of peace on earth when you can't even live at
peace among yourselves? Why don't you fellows
get together first and *then* come out and tell us
how to do it?"

If you feel like saying a hearty "hear hear"
to this question, I would like you to realize that
there are many of us who want to say "Amen"
to it with equal fervour. We Christians are in
no position to point the finger at antagonistic
nations and castes and classes, we stand
condemned alongside everybody else for the
calamitous division in our own ranks, and so
long as Roman Catholic and Protestant, funda-

mentalist and modernist, episcopalian and dissenter, persist in competing with one another like rival firms for a contract, we've little right to be indignant when the man in the street says the Church is a racket just like any other big business. I wish with all my heart that church people would stop thinking of these divisions as if they were just unfortunate, or just regrettable nuisances, and would begin to think of them as *mortal sin*, for that's what they are and that's what the great medieval theologians always declared them to be.

Can you stand a bit of theology for a moment? I want to put this disunity in the Church in its place, the place where the enlightened Christian conscience has always put it. Just as pride is *the* mortal sin of the individual because it cuts a man off from the life of God and so causes his soul to wither and to shrivel, so schism, i.e. division, is the mortal sin of the Church because it cuts each part of the Church, which is the body of Christ, off from the rest and leaves that body broken and lifeless. If I've learnt anything after twenty years of trying to win men and women back to the Church, I've learnt that if the Christian Churches don't hang together they will hang separately. Why, if only the Christians in Germany and in England and in France had stood together in 1914 or in 1939 there would have been no world wars with all their incalculable evils; in our present campaigns for peace and reconstruction we're like an army without a G.H.Q., and the heckler who told me that the Church was really to blame for the fuel crisis was nearer the mark than he realized—a Church without unity sooner or later means a community without power.

The first thing to do about the divisions in the Christian Church is to be ashamed of them, and I am. So I would like to say to the questioner—perhaps we *have* no right to expect you to believe in what we say about love and peace so long as we allow our miserable differences to separate us, but will you come in with us and help us to get rid of them? We *can* offer you one hopeful prospect. We do know at long last *how* we can get together and we have recognized at long last that about certain things we shall never agree, and it wouldn't necessarily be a good thing if we did. We shan't get together by trying to find an agreed formula of belief to which we can all sign along the dotted line. We shan't get together by trying to evolve a form of worship where the Salvation Army and the Anglo-Catholics and the Quakers will all feel equally at home. We shan't get together by trying to turn organized Christianity into a closed shop, and let's not waste our time deploring all this— it isn't worth it. The unity you want to see is a fellowship in *action* rather than a uniformity of doctrine, or ritual, or Church government, isn't it? You don't mind if we train separately, and even think differently, so long as we march together. I agree with you—that's the sort of unity that is desperately needed and I believe we can get it—U.N.O. for the churches with the Lord's Prayer as its charter and no power of veto. We could be so busy seeking the Kingdom of God, and continuing the ministry of Jesus to the poor and sick and outcast, that we hadn't either the time, or the desire to quarrel among ourselves—and we should discover in action how much more there was to unite us than there ever has been to divide us. All too idealistic, do you think? Together with you it could work.

IX

IS THE GOSPEL SIMPLE?

DURING 1946 two of the greatest box office successes in the cinema were both films with a religious theme—"Going My Way" and "The Bells of St. Mary's". Of course their popularity was due to a number of factors that had nothing whatever to do with religion. They were splendidly acted by Bing Crosby, Ingrid Bergman, Barry Fitzgerald, and others, and Bing is much more than a crooner with a really first-class voice, he is an actor of great charm and naturalness. They were brilliantly directed, colourful, human documents; they were spotlessly clean, and they were full of delightful humour. But that's not all. I'm sure a *great*

part of their appeal was that they put over a
view of religion which in itself is popular—
though, as I should want to say, very misleading. Cinemagoers were delighted to see, por-
trayed by Bing Crosby and his straw hat, their
own idea of Christianity as a simple and kindly
faith in a neat and tidy universe—no tiresome
theology, no fleeing from the wrath to come, no
cosmic struggle between good and evil, no great
emphasis on ethical standards even, but just the
art of being kind and the unquestioning assurance that it will all come right by the time
the film ends and the "Pathe Gazette" comes
round. Hollywood had confirmed for them what
they already felt was the "real thing" in religion.

How many times have I been told by hecklers
in Hyde Park that the churches need to get back
to what they call the "simple Gospel of the
Carpenter of Nazareth", and after what I was
saying last week about the divisions in the
Church, and the hopes of unity, one listener at
least thinks that the real reason for our disunity
is that we have got away from the straightforward principle of the golden rule, as he says,
and turned Christianity into a complicated difficult religion which it was never intended to be;
and he wants to know why parsons like myself
don't stop preaching all this controversial stuff
and why we don't get back to fundamentals.

Now I will readily grant the questioner that
some parsons do make religion sound much more
difficult than it is, with their pulpit voices, their

theological jargon and their ponderous sermons, but I can't agree with him that fundamental Christianity is the straightforward principle of the golden rule, and that if you get back to the Carpenter of Nazareth you're getting back to a simple Gospel and a simple creed. This simplification of Christianity is a *myth*, an attractive and kindly myth in the capable hands of Bing Crosby, but a myth. "Going My Way", if it is taken as a portrayal of the Christian life is "Going the Wrong Way"—and what a *lot* of people would have been saved from disillusionment and cynicism if we had been courageous enough to tell them what a complex business living the Christian life turns out to be, how perplexing the golden rule frequently is, how hard it often is to understand what Jesus meant, and what a lot of doubts even the saints have to carry with them alongside their faith.

Beginning to be a Christian is simple enough because you can start where you are—that's one of the marvellous things about Christianity— that's why the faith of a *child* may be real and powerful. I can remember learning to sing "Jesus, Tender Shepherd, hear me, bless Thy little lamb to-night" and feeling quite sure what it meant, and that it was true. But you can't stop there, you can't stay for ever as a "little lamb". There are people I know who reached the "mutton" stage long ago but they are still asking God to treat them as if they were "little lambs" and praying to Him to "make me a good

8

boy" or "make me a good girl". No wonder
their religion is not much better than a super-
stitious relic. For what is childlike and beautiful
at ten years old is childish and silly at thirty.
There's no place for the Peter Pan attitude in
the religious life—as St. Paul said, "you've got
to *grow up* in the faith" and that's a hard and
often painful process. It takes *all you've got* to
follow Jesus Christ, for it is "betting your life",
so to speak, that though there's no ready-made
answer to the personal and national and international problems of to-day they *can* be tackled
and solved in the light of the Gospel, but only
if people like you and me are ready to give our
minds and hearts and wills without reserve to
the job. We shall make mistakes, lose our way,
confess ourselves baffled time and again, but we
shall get there in the end.

x

IS CHRISTIANITY UNIQUE?

I DON'T want you to pity the parson who is
trying to win a verdict from men and women
nowadays for the Christian faith, but I *do* want
you to realize how much more complicated his
task is in the twentieth century than it was for
his predecessors in the eighteenth, for instance.
Broadly speaking, there were only two kinds of

people in England when John Wesley was preaching up and down the country—the good Christians and the bad Christians. You went to church or you stayed away from church, you were a believer or a backslider—there was no other option; but *to-day*, in addition to the problems *within* Christianity itself, there are any number of other religions in the field as well, which makes it all very difficult for the Christian advocate, and all very perplexing, anyhow. Some of you listeners have written to me telling me of the superior qualities of Buddhism and Confucianism—I've had one or two letters from the founders of New Religions altogether, one indeed offering me a partnership, and in all the years during which I have been speaking about Christianity in the open air, one of the most difficult questions to answer has been this question of "comparative religion". Why make such a "to do" about Christianity as if it were the only religion? How do we know that some others aren't better? Christianity may be all right for this country, but Hinduism is probably the best thing for India, just as Judaism is for the Jews, and so on. Now I know that this is far too big a subject for a five minutes talk, for it raises the *ultimate* issues of philosophy and ethics, but I'm sure we Christians can't dodge it, we've got to make some sort of answer that is in simple language and carries conviction. I'll attempt a beginning to that answer by replying to a question sent to me by a Turkish girl who is a

Mohammedan. She asks bluntly, "Do you believe that my religion is as good as yours?"

Well, to begin with I believe that many Mohammedans *live* out their religion just as well as Christians do—and often set an *example* to us by the discipline of their lives and the ardour of their faith. The same is true of Buddhists and Taoists and Jews, yes, and Borneo Head Hunters even! Did you hear Tom Harrison speaking after the nine o'clock news the other Sunday evening? He said that he'd just come back to England after spending some time among these Head Hunters. He'd taken a very kindly view of them, and what seemed to me even more important—they'd taken a very kindly view of him! Mr. Harrison contrasted these so-called savages, who had at least discovered in their primitive religion that there are some things worth dying for, with the people he had met on his return to England, who, despite their avowed Christianity, are living as if there is *nothing* worth dying for. So I should want to say to my Turkish questioner—Christianity has no monopoly of goodness. Your El Ghazali was probably just as good a man as our Christian Francis, or the Hebrew Micah, and it's nothing better than sinful pride to say, "Of course Christianity is better than Mohammedanism or any other religion—just compare the Christians with the infidel Turk and the heathen Chinese." Such a comparison is by no means decisive—and yet I do believe that Christianity is in *itself* the supreme religion, and I'll try to tell you why.

I believe that Jesus Christ is the Way, and the Truth, and the Life as no other teacher or prophet has ever been, and that the Church which is founded upon Him is the highest and best human fellowship, because you'll find in Jesus all the truest and noblest that you can find in the other great religions, but purged of the lower elements which spoil those other faiths. To be a Christian is to learn from the things Jesus Christ put into His gospel what is valuable and true in all the great world religions, and from the things He left out what is false and misleading in them. We are all trying to find God, yes, we are, and we all know a bit what He is like. The spiritual giants, the Buddhas, the Isaiahs and Mahomets, have given us pictures of God each with its truths and its distortions, but all adding immensely to our knowledge of Him—but in Jesus I believe we have the human *photograph* of God—a true speaking likeness. But more even than that I believe that Jesus preaching, healing, dying and rising again, is *God* Himself at work in the world, and I must therefore offer Christianity as the hope of all men everywhere.

XI

THE CHRISTIAN ANSWER TO WAR

THERE are, I've no doubt, many reasons why some of you are *indifferent* to religion as a whole and Christianity in particular, but surely one of those reasons is that in the issue of peace and war, which you regard as the most vital issue of all, you don't think Christianity is any help. You don't think the Church counts one way or the other.

In my experience, when the outsider to Christianity does get into touch with the Church about peace and war, he's much more likely to go to the "Complaints Department" than to the "Enquiry Room", for he feels that he has been let down, and by the very people who professed to know the answer. I wonder sometimes whether you good church folk, who may be listening to me now, realize what a shock it has been to the man in the street to find the majority of Christian people supporting two world wars in twenty-five years. For, strange as it may seem, the one bit of theology that the Church has been able to get over to him is that Christianity is the religion of the meek and lowly Jesus, the Prince of Peace, and whether it is practical politics or not the Church ought to follow in His steps and take the consequences. Time and time again during the last war men said to me on Tower Hill and in Hyde Park, "Christianity and war don't mix—we're not Christians and we've got to fight Hitler and all his gang, but you Christians, you ought to be pacifists—we've no use for bishops blessing battleships and parsons becoming recruiting officers." They had scant respect for our complicated arguments about a "just war" and the "lesser of two evils", and they weren't a bit impressed by our attempt to prove that the end must justify the means—they thought that we had compromised ourselves and we lost their respect.

As one exasperated listener wrote to me after my adverse comments on alcohol the other week, "You Christians are still straining out the gnat and swallowing the camel—denouncing beer and supporting war. Why don't you take your Christianity seriously?" Well, I'll agree with him that it *is* because the world thinks that we are not taking our Christianity seriously that to-day, in all its vital discussions about atomic energy, and its critical conferences about peace-making and the prevention of war, few seem to care what Popes or Archbishops or Moderators have to say, *but* all the same I don't accept this as hopeless. I still believe that the only peace that can come is a Christian peace, just as I believe that the only organization in the world that can outlaw war is the Christian Church, so let me take up an offer made by one listener, and typical, surely, of many more—"Show us

what Christianity can do *now* to prevent another
war and we'd be *really* interested." All right.
Wars happen because there are a sufficient
number of people in almost every country who,
although they know that war is a terrible, dirty,
and wicked business, are prepared under certain
conditions to back it. I am convinced that wars
could *not* happen if there were a sufficient
number of people even in *one* country who were
determined, whatever the circumstances, to
refuse to back a war, as they would refuse to
countenance adultery or commit murder. Who
can make that decision and announce that
refusal and do so straight away? It is my belief,
and I know that I'm in a minority as yet, that
the Christian can and must give that undertak-
ing. He *can*, because he believes that this is
God's world and that therefore it's a moral
universe in which goodness must win and bad-
ness must lose. He must, because his first duty
is to obey God's laws, not to alter them, and he
has the example of Jesus Christ whose triumph
was that He *went on* obeying God when everybody else thought He was an idealistic fool and
a practical failure. I can't argue all this out,
and it's so easy to put difficulties in the way
and say, "Yes, but what would happen if", and
"you can't stand by and let", etc., but it seems
to me that this *is* the way of the Cross and somebody (and who can, except the Christian?),
somebody has got to take it before the world
can rise to a new and tranquil life. I must leave

it there—I can't commit my fellow-Christians, many of whom honestly and intelligently would disagree with my pacifism, but that's where I stand and where I hope one day the whole Church will stand—but we haven't much time.

XII

BEGINNING TO PRAY

I WISH that in these talks I could have answered all the questions that you have sent to me, but there were too many of them. However, thank you for them and I'll do what I can by letter to reply to them. I think I ought to mention the amount of criticism that the talk about the need for a puritan revival provoked, and to say to those who wrote anonymously accusing me of being a "killjoy" that I still think that our greatest danger to-day is the danger of a moral crisis even more than an economic one. But there is one question that I can in all fairness claim is as typical as any of the others about which I've been talking, though of a very different character from them Here it is—"What I'd like to know is this— supposing you are right about Christianity, what do you want us to do—how do you suggest we start to become Christians?"

So let me end these talks with a word about

this practical issue, and I'm all the more concerned to do so because I'm making no bones
about my desire to see you, whoever you are,
doing something, as well as thinking something,
about Christianity in the world to-day. How,
precisely, does a man or a woman who is interested in the proposition that Christianity is the
power to get the right things done, begin to lay
hold of that power and to do them? After all
that must be said about the disagreements
among Christians, here at least we can claim
that Christians of every denomination have
spoken with one voice. *Prayer* is the immediate
technique of faith and power. Praying is the
pipeline along which the Grace of God flows
from Him to you. Now, I well realize that it's
all very well for the Church to say this, but so
many of you feel that either prayer is some
mysterious activity for a few peculiar people and
you can't make head or tail of it, or else if you
think that you understand what it is, you are
just as sure that it doesn't do what it says. And
so you simply don't pray. Now there may be
a hundred explanations as to why you think like
this about prayer, but I want to concentrate on
one of them, and I shouldn't be surprised if it's
the most common. You are thinking of prayer
as the power to get what you want, instead of
the power to do what God wants—trying to get
God on your side rather than trying to get yourself on God's side. Isn't it Dr. Inge who says
that he once received a letter which said: "Dear

Sir: You are a menace—I have prayed for your death. P.S. I have been very successful in two or three previous cases." Of course, you say, that's absurd, but in principle it's no more absurd than asking God to give you the prize in a competition for which you have entered, or even good weather on your holiday, and then when you come bottom or have it rain all the time, assert that God hasn't answered your prayer, and give up praying as a bad job. Incidentally this attitude always prevents you from seeing the simple truth that God may have answered your petition by saying "No" to it. I'm not for a moment saying that you can't tell God how much you'd like that prize, or how much you want that holiday, in fact the more you try to talk to God as a loving and understanding Father the more perfectly will you be praying. The point is that true prayer is the power to change you, not to change God—to change your lives and circumstances by changing your desires and motives, so that you come to want what God wants for you. Now I can't *prove* to you that God is there waiting to hear your prayer, but I can and do say that *I'm* sure He is, and that you can begin to pray to Him whether you've got much faith or little—I'm sure of that too. The next step is with you—it's for you to try it out. Jesus prayed the perfect prayer, and in the days just before Good Friday and Easter I especially invite you to think of it—"If it be possible let this cup (i.e.

the suffering and shame of the cross) pass from me, nevertheless Thy will be done." God didn't answer that prayer by letting Jesus off, but by enabling Him to go through with it. I wish you'd say a prayer like that to-night—I know it will be answered. God bless you.